AUTOB

OF

JOHN G. FEE,

BEREA, KENTUCKY.

[John G. Fee]

INTRODUCTION.

IN consenting to write an introduction to the Autobiography of one whom I have long known and honored, I desire to say that the nineteenth century has not been more remarkable for its discoveries in science, art, and all forms of material progress, than it has for the moral heroism of many men and women whose courage, faith, patience and self-sacrifice have done so much to promote justice and humanity, and for the advancement of the Redeemer's kingdom. Among these Christian patriots there is one whose long life of consecration to the good of his fellow men ought to be not only an example but an inspiration to the youth of our land. John G. Fee, of Berea, Ky., was born and raised under the influences of slavery and was surrounded by those powerfully conservative forces that held many good men to the defense of oppression.

Perhaps no other institution ever did so much to pervert all sense of justice and to deaden all feelings of compassion as that which declares that under a republican government men might hold their unoffending fellow men in bondage.

"Chain them, and task them, and exact their sweat, With stripes that Mercy with a bleeding heart Weeps when she sees inflicted on a beast."

Nay, more, it held that this right of property in man carried with it the right to set at naught the family relation and doom men to the perpetual ignorance of God and his word.

The youth of our land can have little conception of the absolute control that half a century ago the system of slavery had on the minds and consciences of the nation. Nothing but a sublime faith in God enabled the men and women of that day to cheerfully accept reproach, ostracism and ridicule as inevitable consequences of the defense of the poor and needy whose special claim was that they were at once the feeblest and most despised of the children of men. Nor has this been the sole, possibly not the greatest, of the moral conflicts that have demanded and developed a true, moral heroism. The spirit of caste, the outgrowth of slavery, was and is not less exacting and iniquitous. To regard a fellow man simply in his relation to his Maker, and to accord to him just that appreciation that his intelligence and moral worthiness demand, to do this without regard to sect or color, is still held in large sections of our country to be a crime against society which will not be tolerated when there is power to suppress it. So, too, the moral protest against oathbound secret societies,-the uncompromising hostility to the liquor traffic and to any form of legislative approval of it, and above all, the opposition to divisions in the church of Christ as seen in the sects and denominations, demand a moral heroism which needs to be not less steadfast and self-sacrificing than that which wrested from slavery its scepter of power.

Because Mr. Fee was in all these points most uncompromising and true, and because of his indomitable perseverance amidst abounding obstacles, he has achieved a large measure of success, and won the appreciation of even his sometime enemies. But Bro. Fee is now advanced in life. His labor, though still efficient and valuable, cannot in the nature of things much longer continue. His reward is in his works that will follow him. In the language of the poet reformer, John G. Whittier, as applied to another, we may say, "Thanks for the good man's beautiful example."

"His faith and works, like streams that intermingle,
In the same channel ran;
The crystal clearness of an eye kept single
Shamed all the frauds of man.
The very gentlest of all human natures
He joined to courage strong,
And love outstretching unto all God's creatures
With sturdy hate of wrong."

H. H. HINMAN.

PREFACE.

Some six years since a friend requested that I prepare articles for the *Berea Evangelist*, on the topic, "Berea: its History and its Work." I did so. The articles appeared in the *Berea Evangelist* during the years 1885-6. Since that time friends have urged that I prepare a sketch of my leadings and labors up to my coming to Berea, and embody the whole in a volume. To do so will now be labor and care; yet in this way I may be able to do continued good,-utter truth when my tongue shall be silent. I may be able in an emphatic way to say to the reader, *Trust God*-trust him for success, for support, for life. If in this way you will trust God, he by his word, by his Spirit and by his providence, will lead you into the highest usefulness of which, in your day and generation, you are capable. Often trials will come, friends fail, and the heavens above appear as brass and the earth beneath as iron, yet if you will *hold on* with Jacob, or stand still with Moses, you will see the face of God; the Red Sea of difficulties will open before you, and you will walk through dry shod. The future journey may indeed be a barren, stony wilderness, yet the manna will be fresh every morning and the shekinah of God will go before you and lead you across the Jordan, where you will eat the "new corn" in the land of promise. To this my own consciousness bears testimony; were I to say less I would not be faithful.

JOHN G. FEE

Berea, Ky., 1891.

CHAPTER I.

Parentage.-Conversion.-College Life.-At the Theological Seminary.-Deep Conviction and Consecration.-Field of Labor.-Burden of Spirit.-Sealing of the Holy Spirit.-Wife Chosen.-Betrothal.-Search for the Field of Labor.-Marriage.-Called to the Church in Lewis County.-Anti-Slavery Sermon.-Cast out of a Boarding-place.

I WAS born in Bracken County, Kentucky, Sept. 9, 1816.

My father, John Fee, was the son of John Fee, senior. He was of Scotch and English descent. His wife, formerly Elizabeth Bradford, was of Scotch-Irish descent. My father was an industrious, thrifty farmer. Unfortunately he inherited from his father's estate a bondman-a lad bound until he should be 25 years of age.

My father came to the conclusion that if he would have sufficient and permanent labor he must have slave labor. He purchased and reared slaves until he was the owner of some thirteen. This was a great sin in him individually, and to the family a detriment, as all moral wrongs are.

My father was observant, and by his reading kept himself familiar with passing events. He saw that the effects of slavery were bad; that it was a hindrance to social and national prosperity; and consequently invested his money in lands in free States and early deeded portions of these lands to each of his children. He did not see the end from the beginning,-what was to be the after-use of some of these lands.

My mother was industrious and economical; a modest, tender-hearted woman, and a fond mother. I was her first born. She loved me very much, and I loved her in return.

Her mother, Sarah Gregg, was a Quakeress from Pennsylvania. Her eldest son, Aaron Gregg, my wife's grandfather, was an industrious free laborer, an ardent lover of liberty, and very outspoken in his denunciations of slavery. This opposition to slavery and his love of liberty passed to his children and children's children, almost without exception.

In my boyhood I thought nothing about the inherent sinfulness of slavery. I saw it as a prevalent institution in the family life of my relations on my father's side of the house. These were kind to me, and occupied what were considered good social positions. I was often scolded for being so much with the slaves, and threatened with punishment when I would intercede for them. Slavery, like every other evil institution, bore evil fruits, blunted the finest sensibilities and hardened the tenderest hearts.

By false teaching, unreflective youth can be led to look upon moral monstrosities as harmless; as even heaven-approved institutions. Vivid now is the impression made on my youthful mind on seeing a Presbyterian preacher, who was a guest in my grandfather's house, rise before an immense audience and select for his text, "Cursed be Canaan; a servant of servants shall he be unto his brethren." Of course the drift of the discourse was after the plea of the slaveocracy-"God decreed that the children of Ham should be slaves to the children of Shem and Japheth; that Abraham held slaves, and Moses sanctioned such."

All this was intensified by seeing a much venerated neighbor, and slaveholder, who had represented the people in the State Legislature, mount his horse, then uncovering his gray hairs, cry out in a loud voice, "The greatest sermon between heaven and earth." The providence and truth of God led me, in after years, to a very different conclusion.

In the year 1830, when I was fourteen years old, Joseph Corlis, an earnest Christian man, took a subscription school near to my father's house, and insisted with great earnestness that he be allowed to board in my father's family. There was a providence in this. Under his prayers and faithful labors, I was deeply convicted of sin and gave myself to God. My desire was to connect myself with the M. E. church. My father opposed, saying I was too young. He was not himself a Christian. Some two years after this he was awakened, joined the Presbyterian church near to his home, and requested that I go with him. I desired a home with God's people, and gladly embraced the opportunity.

After the lapse of some two years I was impressed that it was my duty to prepare for the Gospel ministry. I soon entered as a student in Augusta College, then located in Augusta, Bracken Co., Ky., my native county. I prosecuted my studies there for about two and a-half years, then went to Miami University, at Oxford, Ohio, and there finished my course of classical study save the review of the last term of study; and finding I could do this at Augusta College, and enter Lane Theological Seminary at the beginning of the term of study there, I returned to Augusta College and took my diploma there. I entered Lane Seminary in the year 1842. Here I met in class one of my former classmates, John Milton Campbell, a former student at Oxford, Ohio. He was a man of marked piety and great goodness of heart. Years previously he had consecrated himself to the work of missions and chose West Africa as his field. Another member of the same class was James C. White, formerly of Boston, Massachusetts, late pastor of the Presbyterian church on Poplar St., Cincinnati. These brethren became deeply interested in me as a native of Kentucky and in view of my relation to the slave system, my father being a slaveholder. They pressed upon my conscience the text, "Thou shalt love the Lord thy God with all thy heart, and thy neighbor as thy self," and as a practical manifestation of this, "Do unto men as ye would they should do unto you." I saw that the duty enjoined was fundamental in the religion of Jesus Christ, and that unless I embraced the principle and lived it in honest practice, I would lose my soul. I saw also that as an honest man I ought to be willing to wear the name which would be a fair exponent of the principle I espoused. This was the name Abolitionist, odious then to the vast majority of people North, and especially South. For a time I struggled between odium on the one hand, and manifest duty on the other. I saw that to embrace the principle and wear the name was to cut myself off from relatives and former friends, and apparently from all prospects of usefulness in the world. I had in the grove near the seminary a place to which I went every day for prayer, between the hours of eleven and twelve. I saw that to have light and peace from God, I must make the consecration. I said, "Lord, if needs be, make me an Abolitionist." The surrender was complete. I arose from my knees with the consciousness that I had died to the world and accepted Christ in all the fullness of his character as I then understood Him. Self must be surrendered. The test, the point of surrender, may be one thing to one man, a different thing to another man; but it must be made,-all given to Christ.

In this consecration-this death to the world-I also made up my mind to accept all that should follow. Imperfect as has been my life, I do not remember that in all my after difficulties I had to consider anew the questions of sacrifice of property, of comfort, of social position, of apparent failure, of personal safety, or of giving up life itself. The latter I regarded as even probable. This, with the rest, had been embodied in my former consecration. I felt that "my life was hid with Christ in God."

Soon after the submission and consecration referred to, the question arose, Where ought I to expend my future efforts, and manifest forth this love to God and man? I had invitations to go with class-mates into the State of Indiana, into communities thrifty and prosperous, with multiplied schools and growing churches. This was enticing to young aspirations, even to those who intended to do good. I was also considering seriously the duty of going with J. M. Campbell, my classmate, to Western Africa; and was in correspondence with the American Board of Commissioners for Foreign Missions in reference to my going as a missionary abroad.

Whilst these fields of labor were being considered, there came irresistibly the consideration of another field: that part of the home field which lay in the South, and especially in Kentucky, my native State. Then came before me my relation to the slave. I had shared in the fruits of his unrequited toil; he was blind and dumb, and there was no one to plead for him.

"Love thy neighbor as thyself" rang in my ears. I also considered the condition of the slave-owner. I knew he was willingly deceived by the false teachings of the popular ministry. I knew also that the great part of the non-slave-owners, who were by their votes and action the actual slaveholders, did not see their crime; that they despised the slave because of his condition, and that these non-slave-owners were violently opposed to any doctrine or practice that might treat the slave as a "neighbor," a brother, and make him equal before the law. I knew also that the great body of the people were practically without the fundamental principle of the Gospel, love to God and love to man; that, as in the days of Martin Luther, though the doctrine of justification by faith was plainly written in the Bible, yet the great body of people did not then see it; so now the great doctrine of loving God supremely and our neighbor as ourselves, "on which hang all the law and the prophets," though clearly written in the Bible, was not seen in its practical application by the great mass of the people. Such was my relation to this people, and theirs to God and the world, that I felt I *must* return and preach to them the gospel of impartial love.

In my bedroom on bended knee, and looking through my window across the Ohio river, over into my native State, I entered into a solemn covenant with God to return and there preach this gospel of love without which all else was "as sounding brass or a tinkling cymbal."

I had kept up correspondence with my father, and told him my convictions and purposes. He was greatly incensed, and wrote, saying, "Bundle up your books and come home; I have spent the last dollar I mean to spend on you in a free State."

At the end of my second year of theological study I returned to my home, intending to do what I could for my father's conversion and that of the family. I spent ten months with my father and the community around. I felt during this time a great burden of spirit in view of the condition of society and the work which lay before me. I spent at one time, alone, in an open field on my father's farm, a whole night in prayer. On two other occasions, in prayer, alone, in a distant part of the farm, I had to my soul two of the fullest revelations of the glory of God in my life's history. These were not my first conversion, nor second conversion, nor sanctification. Conversion is committal to Christ, soul, body, and spirit. Of this I had been conscious previous to these after *sealings* of the Spirit.

Sanctification is none the less by faith than justification, but it is continuous. There may arise to-day a new duty, a new apprehension of a habit un-Christ like, but not seen before. With this new apprehension comes the necessity of a new committal to Christ, with full assurance of sustaining grace.

There was another incident, a providence of good to me in these months of stay and labor. During a series of religious meetings held in the church house where I had previously made my own public profession of Christ, I saw the conversion of the one to whom I gave my best affections, and the one I then decided to make, if possible, the sharer of my future joys and sorrows. I had known her from her childhood, and her mother before her; yet with all her attractions and merits in my eyes, I had no thought of choosing her previous to her conversion, as the partner of my life. I knew no one could be happy with me, nor a help-mate in the life I had resolved to live, unless she was converted, and thus one in *spirit* and *purpose* with myself.

On that day of her conversion and espousal to Christ (for I heard her experience and consecration) I decided to seek with her future oneness. I had before me a *governing purpose*, and to this all my plans conformed. Marriage to me was not a mere impulse nor a mere business transaction. I believed then, as now, that in order to true and wise marriage there is some one in the world in whom there is, first, that peculiar combination of qualities which form the basis of peculiar and exclusive affection; and then there must be that purpose of soul and habit of life that fit for future harmony and usefulness. This I found in her: that affection, sympathy, courage, cheer, activity, frugality and endurance, which few could have combined, and which greatly sustained me in the dark and trying hours that attended most of our pathway. This much is due to truth and may be suggestive to others.

By this time it became apparent that my work in trying to convert my father to sentiments of justice and liberty was ended. He had supplied himself, from every possible source, with pro-slavery books and pamphlets, and became violent in his opposition to all efforts for the freedom of the slave. He still hoped to efface my convictions and lure me from my purpose. He offered to pay all bills if I would go to Princeton, New Jersey, and spend a year in the Theological Seminary in that place. This offer I declined. I said, I will not by any act of mine bid God-speed to an institution in which the teaching and practice is subversive of the fundamental principles of the Gospel,-love to God supreme, and to our neighbors as ourselves.

I was offered the pastorate of two churches in the county (Bracken), with abundant support, but on the condition that I would "go along and preach the Gospel and let the subject of slavery alone." I replied, "The Gospel is the good news of salvation from sin, all sin, the sin of slave-holding as well as all other sins; and I will not sell my convictions in reference to that which I regard as an iniquity, nor my liberty to utter these convictions for a mess of pottage."

I saw that my work in that region was ended. But my covenant was upon me to preach the gospel of love in Kentucky. I needed therefore to look for another field.

Ecclesiastically I was connected with the New School Presbyterian "church" or sect. The ministerial brethren of that body at that time, in Kentucky, were relatively few. Several of these brethren earnestly solicited my co-operation. I told them my convictions in reference to the sinfulness of human slavery; of its utter subversion of the great fundamental principles of the Gospel. Some replied, "Yes, slavery is a bad thing; so was polygamy; but God tolerated it, and sent his prophets to preach principles that ultimately supplanted it. So," they said, "we must deal with slavery." I replied,

Principles can be effective only as they are seen and applied.

I was fettered with the notion that if I would purify the church, or sect, I must stay in it and there apply the principles, hold up the truth. Soon, however, an "eye-opener"

came. I was invited to attend a meeting of the presbytery within the bounds of which I was then living. This was near to Cynthiana, Harrison Co., Ky. I went. I saw there, as elsewhere, the blight of slavery on every thing around me; the degradation of the slave, the idleness of the youth, the pride of the people, the spirit and manner of the ministers themselves. Sabbath came; and the hour to commune, to eat at the Lord's table, came. With this came to my mind the text, "If any man that is called a brother be a fornicator, or covetous, or an idolater, or a railer, or a drunkard, or an extortioner; with such an one not to eat." I said, If the slaveholder be not an extortioner, then no man under heaven is. I left the church house, and went out into an adjoining woodland and sat down on a log and wept as I thought of my condition,-that of holding ecclesiastical connection with men with whom I could not eat at the Lord's table. The pastorate of that church was offered to me. I saw in the eldership and leading members determined opposition to the freedom of the slave. I saw there was not to me, in that place, an open door, and returned to my home.

After a few days I took my horse and started on an exploring tour through the interior of the State. Then, like most other ministers, I was working in the narrow groove of sect, and that a small one in Kentucky. Going from place to place, I traveled on horseback between three and four hundred miles. I heard, in my journeying, of a small church in the city of Louisville, Kentucky, then without a pastor. I visited the church and found the membership small-twenty-one in number. In this church there was to me one hopeful feature, and that was that there was but one slave-owner in the membership, and she the widow of a former preacher, who was represented as having been an anti-slavery man. I said, This people will probably hear the truth spoken in love. I agreed to come and labor with them for a season. I then returned to my home in Bracken County.

Soon a letter from the church followed me, saying, "If you will be useful among us, you must separate yourself from that abolition presbytery at Cincinnati." By that presbytery I had been licensed to preach the Gospel, and my connection, ecclesiastically, was yet with that body. I replied, If my usefulness with you depends upon my separating from godly men, then with you I cannot be useful.

Again I was apparently without a field of labor; but my purpose was unchanged, and my willing covenant to preach the gospel of love in my native State was yet upon me, but in what place to preach

I knew not. With me it was then true that I must go forward, "not knowing whither I went."

As previously suggested, my life's future was merged with that of another, and hers with mine: She had decided to go where I should go, and if I roamed in keeping my covenant, I should not roam alone. Accordingly with her consent, Matilda Hamilton and I were married September 26, 1844.

Soon after this, two brethren, S. Y. Garrison and E. P. Pratt, extended to me an invitation to assist in a meeting to be held in Lewis County, Kentucky. I accepted the invitation and went at the time appointed. I found a new church house just completed, and a large concourse of people. As I was informed, most of the people were descendants of Pennsylvanians, and but few slave-holders were in the community. The membership of the church was small, but to me hopeful. There were at the beginning of the meeting only three members. These were women, wives of men who were not slave-holders. During the meeting two persons, on the profession of their faith, were added to the church. These were not slave-holders. I preached to the people, found attentive ears, and immediately an urgent solicitation to labor with them.

In that community there was but one other church, a small band of Old School Presbyterians. The man who preached to them, once in each month, lived many miles distant, and was pro-slavery in his teachings. I said, These people are practically without the Gospel; this is missionary ground; there is an open door and I will come. Efforts were made to secure for me a partial support. Nearly one hundred dollars were pledged by the people; application was made to the American Home Missionary Society for additional aid; and, as I now recollect, the sum was two hundred dollars. I returned to Bracken County, where I had previously left an appointment to deliver a lecture on the subject of slavery, in the court house in Brooksville the county seat. This appointment produced great commotion. Threats of violence were made, and with these came entreaties from relatives and friends to withdraw the appointment. During life, in all new or responsible engagements, I have been slow and careful in making them; but once made, as far as I can now remember, I have met my appointments, or made a vigorous effort in trying to do so.

I went to the appointment,-my wife with me. James Hawkins, then the nominal slave of my father-in-law, went also, but "followed afar off." He went not to be seen as a hearer, but to guard the horses and saddles of myself and wife, and this of his own devising;-not known to us. We found in the court house a small audience of men. I delivered my lecture and we came quietly home.

My father was so incensed that he said, "Enter not my door again." After some two weeks I preached a sermon in Sharon church house. My father was present. After sermon he invited me and Matilda, my wife, to go home with him. Though he opened, for a time, the door of his house, he never opened the door of his heart to the sentiments of freedom to the slave, or to the doctrine of doing unto men as he would they should do unto him.

The prospects of the newly-begun life, to my wife, were not flattering, and all I could then do was to walk by faith and not by sight. After the lapse of a few more weeks we went to Lewis County, to enter upon the work as previously arranged. We took board in the house of Benjamin Given. He was a member of the M. E. Church.

Soon after entering upon my work in Lewis County, John D. Tully, then husband to Ruth Tully, who was a member of the little church, requested that I would preach a sermon on the subject of slavery. I at once consented, and announced my purpose to do so at Union church house, four weeks from that time. I had then an engagement to attend in the meantime, the then-called "Southwestern Anti-slavery Convention," to be held in the city of Cincinnati, Ohio, in the month of April, 1845. At that convention I made my first acquaintance with Salmon P. Chase, and was with him on the committee of resolutions there discussed and adopted. There I heard George W. Clark sing in his inimitable manner, that soul-stirring song, "Be free! O man, be free!" There I heard read a letter of great eloquence and power from Elihu Burritt, for whom I afterward named my firstborn son, Burritt.

I returned to Lewis County, Kentucky, my then chosen field of labor. At the appointed time I went to the church house where I had engaged to preach a sermon on the subject of slavery. I found there more people than could be seated in the house. I selected the text, "Thou shalt love the Lord thy God with all thy heart, and with all thy soul, and with all thy mind, and thy neighbor as thyself." I showed that human slavery was plainly a violation of this fundamental principle of the Christian religion. I then considered the various texts in the Old and New Testaments assumed as sanctions of slavery. I showed that such assumptions were wrong; that the precepts of Christianity must be construed in harmony with its fundamental principles, and that slavery was sinful as certainly as anything in human action could be sinful. I invited the congregation to come back the next Lord's day and we would then consider the various schemes for the removal of this evil; I then dismissed them.

On the next Lord's day the congregation was not so large as on the previous occasion. I reminded my audience that we had shown on the previous occasion that human slavery was a violation of the law of love, and therefore a sin; that this sin, like all other sins, needed to be repented of, and that immediately; just as we should immediately repent of any other great sin. I then considered the plea for colonization. I showed that to banish a man from the land of his birth, guilty of no crime, was gross injustice-only adding iniquity to crime. I showed that to do right is always safe; and that emancipation in the West Indies was an acknowledged good to all;

that the slaves in our country, as a general rule, were patient, long-suffering, receptive, trusting, and, withal, acclimated; and would be more quiet laborers than those we would import from abroad. The verdict was soon rendered: "He is an Abolitionist, in favor of 'nigger' equality; his teaching is dangerous to our property, and will breed insurrection and rebellion; he ought to be moved."

That Sabbath afternoon was not a quiet one in that part of Lewis County where we then were. No violence as yet; only jeers and taunts. My wife was as quiet as if all around her had been serene. The next morning our landlord informed me that his wife was unwilling to keep us any longer. We had not a home of our own. My covenant was still on me to spread the gospel of love, justice and mercy, in Kentucky, my native State; where, I knew not. My purpose was unchanged. I could only stand still and see the salvation of God. It came.

CHAPTER II.

A Home.-Resolutions of the Church.-Salary.-Meeting of Synod.-Resolutions.-My Withdrawal.-Ecclesiastical Position.-Union on Christ.-Separation from A. M. Society.-Anticipated Mob.-Prosecution of Hannahs.-Invitation to C. M. Clay.-Expected Violence.-Anti-Slavery Manual.-Protest against Secret Orders.

MONDAY morning found us absolutely without a home. My wife picked up her bonnet and went across the stream, Cabin Creek, to the house of "Uncle" Robert and "Aunt" Lydia Boyd. They were "Disciples"-disciples indeed. My wife said to Aunt Lydia, "We are without a home; can we stop with you for a few weeks?" The reply was, "Certainly; come in." In a sense we were "strangers," and "they took us in." In less than two hours our little effects were removed and we were under another roof.

I said to my wife, "My covenant is upon me to stay in Kentucky and preach this gospel of love. If I do so I must have a home of my own, a place where I shall be a fixture, a taxpayer; have a claim to citizenship and protection." I had 409 acres of land in northern Indiana which I could then sell for six dollars per acre. I sold half of the tract and bought half of an acre of ground adjoining the lot of the friend with whom we were stopping. I found two men who said they would build for me a house if they had to "hold the sword in one hand and the trowel in the other; the pistol in one and the saw in the other." These were ungodly men-"the earth helped the woman." To secure material, even for a small house, was then, to me, a tedious business. Some of this lumber had to be hauled ten miles-not by railroad, or on turnpikes, but on jolt wagons and over mud roads.

After some weeks my wife and I, "on horseback," went twenty-five miles to the house of her parents, where she tarried a few weeks, until our first child was born.

I immediately returned to my field of labor, filling appointments from Sabbath to Sabbath. My audiences were small, ranging from eight to twelve persons. Two persons who had united with the original three, went back as soon as persecutions arose. Two others, converted by the power of truth and Spirit of God, were added. These endured until death called them away. The church at a regular meeting resolved to treat slave-holding as they would any other practice plainly contrary to the Word of God, and refuse church fellowship to all persisting in the practice of slave-holding. I continued my appointments at Union Church house and at private houses where I could find an open door. The one hundred dollars, pledged toward my support, were ciphered down to twenty-five. One of the preachers, who knew my condition, and had known me for many years, had often been at my father's house. He had urged me to go to that field, and had pledged twenty-five dollars of the one hundred promised for my support, but when he heard I had uttered my convictions in sermons against human slavery, he declined to pay what he had pledged, saying "he had intended to give to me a colt worth twenty-five dollars, but it had died"; "moreover, if I should find myself taken out some night, ridden on a rail and ducked in a pond, I would receive only what my folly deserved." This action of his need not now be surprising when we consider that this man had a rich farm, in an adjoining county, worked by slaves, and the women were driven to the hempfield whilst their babes lay crying on the kitchen floor. This I saw in passing. To some it will now seem horrid that I should have had any ecclesiastical association with such a man. I did not long retain such.

In the month of October, 1845, I attended the annual meeting of the Synod of Kentucky, Presbyterian, New School, at Paris, Ky. The Synod in reviewing the records of Ebenezer Presbytery considered the action of the church in Lewis Co., of which church I was then pastor. The church had by a unanimous vote declared that they would regard slave-holding as a sinful practice-a plain violation of the law of God, and refuse church fellowship to those persisting in the practice of slave-holding. This action was pronounced unwarranted and my part in it as reprehensible.

A prominent member of the Synod and its Corresponding Secretary immediately entered upon a defense of slave-holding, and this in the light of Bible teaching, and with this a severe reflection upon me for teaching the opposite doctrine. In reply I gladly accepted the discussion of the subject of slavery, and that in the light of the Bible. After the second round the moderator decided we must not discuss the subject in the light of the Bible, but in the light of the constitution of the church, the "denomination to which we belonged." I replied, even in the light of this constitution slavery is wrong. This constitution declares an offense to be "any thing in the principle or practice of a church member which is contrary to the Word of God; or which, if it be not in its own nature sinful, may lead others to sin or mar their spiritual edification." I said, as we have shown, slave-holding is contrary to the Word of God, violates the law of love in taking away natural rights, and also tempts others to sin. The discussion was stopped by the moderator. A peroration was given by a venerable member, Dr. C_____, who said, "If the young man shall find himself some day taken out, ridden on a rail and ducked in a pond, he need not be surprised."

The Synod then passed four resolutions.

1. "That the action of the church in Lewis County, in declaring slave-holding as sinful, and refusing church fellowship to slave-holders, is unwarranted.

2. The action of Bro. Fee in aiding and encouraging such action is censurable in thus disturbing the peace of Zion, and in breaking his covenant vows to study the peace of Zion.

3. That the A. M. Society be requested not to give aid to him as an evangelist in our midst.

4. That Ebenezer Presbytery be requested to appoint a committee to visit and labor with the church in Lewis County." The committee came not.

At the next meeting of the Synod, which meeting was held at Midway, Ky., my action in connection with the church in Lewis Co., Ky., was again taken up. I had said to the brethren of the Synod I had believed it to be my duty to stay with my brethren for a time and do what I could to induce them to cease from the practice or sanction of the sin of slave-holding. A prominent member replied: "A man may hold a black-eyed pea so near his eye that he will shut out of vision the whole world." Application was made.

It was then said, "On our part there is no hope for repentance, and you have done all you can unless it be by withdrawing and consistently going where you belong." It was then added, "The constitution of the church," the denomination, "to which you belong says nothing against slavery and it is your duty to construe the constitution of the church as the body you belong to construes it." I replied, "It is now manifest that my work with you is done. Also, the position you assume is practical popery; you interpose between me and the Word of God a human creed and then demand that I construe that creed as the body to which I belong construes it. This takes away the right of private interpretation. This is the very essence of popery." I said, "Give to me a letter of dismission." This they did, as "in good and regular standing save agitation of the slavery question." With this separation ended, on my part, all direct connection with slave-holding bodies.

As it now is, my work has been small, but had I consented to remain in the Synod of Kentucky, and to pursue the policy advised and adopted by the brethren in that Synod, my work would have been an utter failure. So far as I now know every church that consented to the conservative position, yea, proscriptive position of that Synod, has gone down. It either died for want of life or went over to the Old School body in its unqualified fellowship of slaveholders. This failure was not to be attributed to want of ability in the ministry. Such men as Clelland, Gallaher Dickerson, Mills, Pratt and others were men of acknowledged ability. The majority of the ministers acknowledged the wrong of slavery in comparing it to concubinage, but said it was to be worn out by preaching principles. These brethren were negative, conservative. The slave power was positive, aggressive, and wore out these conservative ministers and their churches. When sins are gross and incorporated into the organic law of the land, nothing short of unqualified condemnation and refusal to support will be sufficient.. Ministers must speak out as Nathan to David, "Thou art the man." "The blood of a murdered man lies at your door." "Put away the evil of your doings." Nothing short of such faithfulness will ever succeed.

An important question was now before us as a church-what ecclesiastical position shall we assume? what shall we do for ecclesiastical co-operation? We had a lingering feeling somewhat like that of the children of Israel in the days of Samuel, when they said: "We must be like the nations round about us." But God led and taught us otherwise.

We saw that to succeed in Kentucky we must have the co-operation of all true Christians, who trusted in Christ as their Savior from sin-all sin. Bro. G. came across the Ohio river and said, "Bro. Fee, we Free Presbyterians have so amended our Confession of Faith that we shut out all slave-holders; join with us." I said: "To do so would leave us but a little handful in Kentucky; also there are good brethren here who would not like your creed, in other respects; nor the name Presbyterian.

Bro. W., a Wesleyan of good ability and of true piety, came. He said: "Bro. Fee, Wesleyans have no connection with slave-holding and our creed is small; join with us." I said: "We are glad of your protest against slave-holding and hope your creed will grow still smaller so that it will shut out no true child of God who accepts Christ in all the fullness of his character; but there are brethren here who would not like to accept your creed nor take the name Wesleyan." We said that it is manifest that in order to success we must have a creed so simple that all true followers of Christ can unite on it. And we must have a name so catholic that all the true followers of Christ can wear it. This must be

Christian as designating individual character; and church of Christ at _____ as designating the local church. Thus were we led by the logic of events to see the wisdom of the plan long before marked out by our Lord when he said: "Neither pray I for these alone, but for all them that believe on me through their word, that they may be one."

The basis of union was Christ, a person-not opinions-but a PERSON. "Other foundation can no man lay than is laid, which is Jesus Christ." The reason for fellowship was manifested faith in Christ as the Savior from sin. On this foundation came together those who had been known as Presbyterians, Disciples, Methodists and Baptists.

A question now arose in my mind as to the propriety of my receiving aid from the American Home Missionary Society. I gave to the Society my reasons why I must decline further aid: They were as follows:

1. In securing and sending an annual contribution to your Society I will thereby help sustain and build up slave-holding.

2. However small my influence may be, my continued reception of your aid would be thus far an endorsement of your policy; this I may not give.

The society replied they thought I ought to be satisfied if they were willing to give aid to me in my protest against slave-holding; and in reference to pastors aided, their work of inquiry was ended when the pastors are regarded as "rectus in ecclesia," "right in church." This was Congregationalism "with a vengeance."

I replied: "Christ is not the minister of sin and you ought not to be, and I may not help you in this."

Just at this time, Jan. 17, 1846, Bro. A. A. Phelps, who was secretary of the Union Missionary Society, merged soon after this into the American Missionary Association, wrote to me saying, "I think you should stay where you are and itinerate three or six months, as you can. I hope you will, on no account, withdraw your application for a re-commission from the Home Missionary Society; if they refuse, they make Abolitionism a test of church standing as Dickerson has in his refusal to recommend you. Do not let them off-urge and insist on a decision of the 'new case.'"

The Society did not want to be "let off."

I felt I must let them off. Whilst they manifestly, for some reason, desired to help sustain one anti-slavery church in the South they were at the same time sustaining fifty two slave-holding churches in the South. This was blowing hot and cold-serving God and the devil-doing evil on a large scale, that good might come on a small scale. I said: "I may not bid you God speed in your wicked policy," and returned their commission.

The little church established on the one foundation, Christ, and its pastor disenthralled from all slave-holding alliances, and the little cottage now enclosed, one room with one coat of plastering on and that not dry, the humble pastor, wife and first-born child entered. With a small case of books on the right, a small cupboard on the left, our little Laura in a cradle in the middle, a bed behind, at nightfall Matilda and I sat down before a cheerful fire in an open fireplace, without a cloud of the unseen future before us.

In this little room sixteen feet square, with bed and table extending a plank from one chair to another, we had preaching Sunday evenings after I returned from distant appointments. Monday morning whilst I made fires, fed the horse and milked the cow, my wife swept out dirt from previous muddy shoes and scrubbed out stains from tobacco spit as far as she could. The one end to be attained, at whatever sacrifice, was the lodgment of fundamental truth in the minds of the people.

As we began to plant ourselves more fixedly in the State, the slave power busied itself in efforts to stir up opposition and mob violence. A plot was arranged to waylay me on my way to an appointment some fifteen miles distant. Some men who were friends proposed to go and defend me from assailants; but said they would not go without arms. I said: "I carry no weapons; I know retaliation will destroy society. If I suffer I will make my appeal to the civil courts." These friends declined going. My wife said she would go. The babe was left with a kind neighbor woman.

Saturday morning found Matilda and me each on horseback, winding our way through the hills of Lewis to our appointment fifteen miles distant on the banks of the Ohio river. No molestation that day. That night during the hour of preaching some "roughs" took our horse out of the stable, took him off into the forest, tied some billets of wood to his tail and started him, thinking he would be greatly frightened and they see some fun. "Ben" took the matter so gently that they declared he had "religion" and let him go at pleasure. When my wife found that her horse was gone, the horse her father had given to her, and that he was probably being abused, she was troubled and "sweat at the eyes." Old Father Rankin, John Rankin, had come across the Ohio river to attend the meeting; and byway of comfort to my wife, said: "Why, Sister Fee, I have had my horse's tail shaved and mane cropped and one ear cut off, and he rode just as well afterward as before." Not long after "Ben" was found quietly browsing among the bushes and waiting to do his part in further evangelization.

The next day it was confidently asserted assault would be made on our way home. The proposed assault, however, had been disconcerted by the sudden death of the leader, who was killed in a saw-mill. As angry members of the proposed mob two men waylaid us, but were hindered from personal violence by the presence of a sturdy farmer, who had purposely planned to return home with us. One of the assailants, with a club in hand, rode rapidly up to me in a threatening attitude; but my wife, dexterous on horseback as he, at each moment interposed herself between me and H. After two or three passes, the sturdy farmer rode up and said: "Hannahs, if you do not clear out from here, I will get down and beat you till there shall not be a sound bone in your body." Hannahs contented himself by dismounting and throwing stones, one of which struck me, but without serious injury to me.

Whilst not seriously injured, I saw this was my opportunity to show, that whilst I did not avenge personal injury I would show respect to civil law by appealing to it for protection and gaining, if possible, a decision of the courts in favor of free speech and personal security. I brought the case before the grand jury, and through that into the circuit court.

The judge was a slaveholder. He said to the court: "Gentlemen, Mr. Fee is an Abolitionist, and if slave-holding is sinful, then the Abolitionists are right. They say, repent of sin immediately; and you would not say to pickpockets, quit your sin gradually." But having called for a Bible, he opened it and said: "Slavery is not sinful; the Bible sanctions it," and referred to the case of Abraham, and the instruction of Moses to buy of the heathen round about, and of Paul as returning Onesimus, "a runaway slave." Closing the book, he said: "But, gentlemen, free speech must be had; and Mr. Hannahs ought to be ashamed of his conduct, and the court must fine him."

This decision gave to me a measure of protection in Lewis County, but did not wholly suppress the spirit of violence in adjoining counties.

About this time, at my suggestion, a petition was sent to Cassius M. Clay, requesting him to come to Lewis County, July 4th, 1846, and make to us an address on the subject of slavery and emancipation. The call was signed by twenty-seven citizens, to be sent to Mr. Clay.

Mr. Clay accepted the invitation, commended highly the courage of the men who had made the call, but sent back the sad intelligence that he must defer the purposed address until his return from the war with Mexico.

Accompanying this call went the letter of a neighbor, saying: "The anti-slavery sentiment of the community will soon be embodied, and it will be made known that no man, Whig or Democrat, can have their votes who is a practical slaveholder, or an apologist for slavery." This was sent to Mr. Clay and published in the True American. This stirred the slave power, especially in Mason County, the adjoining county. An article appeared in the Maysville Eagle, which in some respects misrepresented the statement of the former, by saying: "This is as rank Abolitionism as was ever uttered by Birney or Tappan. No slaveholder is hereafter to receive the votes of these simon-pure liberty men; and they who dare to apologize for the institutions of our country are thus denounced and proscribed, and this is heralded forth as the sentiments of Lewis County." This was a misrepresentation. The sentiments only of those organized were declared.

Mr. Clay, having declined then to come, and the slave power raging, some ten men of the twenty-seven who had signed the call inviting Mr. Clay to come, took back their names; and upon myself, Mr. Clay's correspondent, were gathered the severest anathemas, and threats of violence and of the utter destruction of my house. The night for the work of desperation was fixed. My friends expected the threatened violence, and a man whom we knew as a friend and one who had opportunity to know the movements of our enemies came three times during the day and entreated that I leave my home or I would certainly be killed. At night we went to bed as usual. The night was one of terrific darkness, thunder and lightning. Many, with purposes of violence, did gather at the place of rendezvous, but dispersed before the frowning elements. Soon after this the prime mover was killed by a tenant. The slain man, though a major, a slaveholder with large property, was so little esteemed by his neighbors that, as I was informed, scarcely enough gathered to give to him a decent burial. Another man who shot at me whilst I was sitting in my house, was soon afterward drowned in the Ohio river.

For reasons manifest my audiences were small. Many whose sympathies were with the principles of justice and liberty were afraid to be seen listening to me in public audiences. I saw I must try and reach the people at their homes, at their firesides; and I decided I would write and publish an anti-slavery manual, a hand-book showing the testimony of God's Word against slavery,-the evil consequences of slavery upon society, and with these show the unity of the human race-that verily "God hath made of one blood all nations of men." The matter for this manual I prepared, and, for best effect, decided to publish in Kentucky,-in Maysville, a city near by.

Whilst preliminary arrangements were being made, a man of wealth and influence in that city wrote to me a letter, saying that if I should come to that city and attempt to publish an anti-slavery book he would head a band of sixty men, ride me on a rail and duck me in the Ohio river. I went on with my publishing, and attended to proof-reading there in the city. Whilst there the conductor of the press said to me: "My father, Judge Chambers and John A. McClung, will this forenoon make speeches in the court house. Come, go down." I went.

I had a few days previously headed a petition to Congress praying that Texas might be admitted as a free State and thus delivered from slavery, which our own statesman, Henry Clay, admitted to be a curse. As the meeting was about to adjourn, a little fellow, a practicing attorney at the bar, well known as Tom Payne, jumped to his feet and said: "There is a matter here that ought to be now attended to. There is," said he, "a certain man by the name of John G. Fee up here in the edge of Lewis County, who has headed a petition to Congress in which he denounces Henry Clay, the son of Kentucky. It is time such men were silenced and driven out of the county." As he ended this sentence, I arose to my feet, and addressing the chairman, Judge Reed, the noted defender of slavery and free speech previously referred to, said: "Mr. Chairman, I happen to know something about that petition. I drafted it and know that Henry Clay is not denounced. So far as he is concerned, his words are commended."

Cries went up: "Take him out; take him out." Instantly almost the whole house arose to their feet. Some tried to get me into the aisle. I refused. I knew that was not the place of security to me. A stout man, a stone-mason, stepped to my side, and with an uplifted, brawny arm, said: "Men, I have been in one war (1812), and will be in another before this man is taken out." He knew me.

Judge Reed, with stentorian voice, cried out: "Sit down, men, sit down. I would be ashamed to preside in a meeting where a man is publicly assailed and yet not allowed a word in defense. One of old said: 'Though you slay me, hear me.' Speak on, speak on." I did so, and the audience dispersed quietly. We here scored another count for free speech and personal security.

I went on with the publication of my book, and distributed with my own hands many copies in the city.

Afterward the American Missionary Association abridged the book and distributed many copies in this and other States.

I wrote, for more general distribution, a tract on the sinfulness of slave-holding; another on the duty of non-fellowship of slaveholders in church relationship, and another on the folly of colonization as a plan of emancipation.

Just about this time the occasion for another protest came,-a protest against secret orders. We had a union temperance society, into which all, young and old, rich and poor, could come, "without money and without price."

It was proposed that there be formed in our school-house a society known as "Sons of Temperance." I was requested to join and give my influence. I declined the invitation to join, and in a public discourse gave my reasons for so declining.

First, impracticable. The form of organization-initiation fees, with passwords and closed doors,-such will shut out a large portion of society, will fail to meet the needed end,-the reclamation of the masses.

Second, the secret principle is wrong. (1) It is contrary to the genius of republican institutions, where every movement affecting the interests of society is supposed to be open to the view of all.

2. Unfair. Such societies being secret, give one class of men an unknown and an undue advantage over the other members of society,-an unfair advantage.

3. Dangerous. Such societies give opportunities not only for unfair advantages, but opportunities to bad men to devise measures not only injurious to society but perilous to governments. Such sad experiences have occurred.

4. Such societies are selfish, and as such, contrary to the spirit and letter of Christianity. (1) They reject the very objects of charity-"the halt, the lame, the blind,"-help those who help the society and can help themselves. (2) Usually they reject men in this country simply because they are colored. This fosters the spirit of caste. (3) This society, as such, hides from the world whatever light or good it may have,-"puts it under a bushel." Christianity requires that we let our light shine; if we have good works let them be seen. If there be any thing good, society ought to have the benefit of it. (4) This was the precedent of our Lord, who said: "I spake openly in the temple, and in secret have I said nothing." He is our pattern.

It was then said: "The amount of secrecy is small." I said, the principle is just as certainly vicious when small as when large; a poison is the same, little or much. I said the devil tempts not to vice in its gross form: at first only in small proportions, and that veiled by some assumed good; "he comes as an angel of light." I said: "Some of you know that it is just in this way Jesuitism now works. It does evil that good may come."

I said, "I have traced the history of your movement. It was concocted almost exclusively by Free-masons and Odd-fellows." These men knew that temperance was a good and reputable thing, and that if the youth of the land could have their minds familiarized with the secret principle, made reputable by association with acknowledged good, then it will be easy, after a time, for such to step into other orders with larger measures of secrecy, even those associated with blasphemous oaths, a false religion, a religion like that of Free-masonry, which claims to fit men for the lodge above,-"a religion in which all men can agree,"-Jews and pagans, Mohammedans and Parsees; a religion of mere sacrilegious rites; a religion in which the name of Christ is excluded from every official prayer; Christ treated as Mohammed, Zoroaster or Confucius; yes, worse, the name expurgated from Scriptures quoted.-See Mackey's Ritual, pp. 384-5. I said to my hearers: "Beware of those stepping stones that lead to institutions that are blaphemous, delusive, and perilous to society and republican institutions."

The "Sons" did not live long in that region. Afterwards, when I had moved to Madison Co., where I now live, I was told by an influential friend, who was a Free-mason, that if I would join the Masons I would be protected from the mobs. I replied: "If my protection and immunity from violence is to be secured by connection with orders at once delusive, selfish, perilous to society and treacherous to Christ, then I cannot have protection from such men." Before I came to Madison, I was waylaid, shot at, clubbed, stoned; by force kept out of church houses; and since I came to Madison, have been in the hands of six regularly organized mobs of violent men, yet have I not shown the secret sign of distress, nor muttered the words, "Is there no help for the widow's son?"

I have by these persecutions been brought into deeper sympathy with Him whose judgment was taken from Him and who said: "Blessed are ye when men shall revile you and persecute you, and say all manner of evil against you falsely for my sake." His gracious benediction was more than the maledictions of men. I yet live, and live to praise Him for that abundant grace which, like the "red thread," has run through the cordage of my life.

CHAPTER III.

Commission from the A. M. A.-Preaching and Church Building.-Redemption of a Slave Woman.-Her Effort to Free her Children.-Her Capture and Imprisonment.

IN 1848 I received a commission from the American Missionary Association-appropriation $200, as I now remember. Previous to this, for more than a year, my wife and I had lived on our own small resource. My wife was industrious; and I believe no man ever accused me of being idle. Aside from necessity, we had resolved that we would not only advocate free labor, but also, as far as we could, we would dignify labor by the work of our hands.

By this time we had a little frame house built by the community to be used as a school-house and church house. The Lord granted to us a manifestation of his presence. Twenty-one persons were converted, a prayer meeting and Sunday-school sustained.

In this year, 1848, I began regular preaching in Bracken County, my native country and the native country of my wife. The place for preaching was in a school-house, distant from my home in Lewis twenty-five miles. To this appointment I came every second week. Here Wm. Goodell visited us and preached two or three sermons. I continued regular preaching. The first person who there came forward to confess Christ, was my mother-in-law, Elizabeth Hamilton. Next came John D. Gregg, her brother, a faithful man. One after another came. In process of time came Mary Gregg, mother of the first two who came. She had secured to a bondman a deed of emancipation before she joined the church. Thus the testimony of the church was kept clear from any appearance of connivance at any form of oppression.

Soon it became manifest that we must have a larger house. We decided to build. We were all of one mind that the highest security demanded that we build a brick house. We so decided. I asked the question: "Shall the seats be free?" The question was apparently a surprise. One after another said: "Certainly." "But," I said, "do you mean what you say?" The reply was: "We suppose we do." I said: "If when the house shall be erected, a colored man, free or slave, shall come in and seat himself as any other man, where he thinks he can hear to the best advantage, will that with you be all right?" John D. Gregg said, "Yes;" some others said "Yes." After a silence a good brother whose probity was known all over the county, said: "Bro. Fee, that is my rule in my house; and when Billie C____ comes in he sits down at my table as I do; but in a place of public worship as you here propose, you cannot do this. If you attempt it one brick will not be left on another." I said, "In the light of your own example to do so is right, is it not?" "Yes, Bro. Fee; but all things that are lawful are not expedient." I said: "In mere measures, that may often be true, but in questions of morals-a religious movement like this-it will be wise to do what is confessedly right." He then said he had subscribed $100, and would now leave $50 for us to try with. Another took back part of his subscription. Others increased theirs. A young man then living in the community, an earnest, active Abolitionist who loved to buttonhole every conservative preacher he could get his hands on, said, "You put up the walls and I will put on the roof." The walls went up, and I.B.C. put on the roof. The little brick church yet stands. At the end of entrance, above the doorways, is a white marble slab, placed there by John D. Gregg; and of his own devising are inscribed these words, "Free Church of Christ." The sentiment it expressed was, church of Christ, undemoninational, free to all men.

The church was blessed. A generation of young people was raised up there who, with their children, and even children's children, have gone out to disseminate sentiments there learned and to bless society wherever they have gone. The church there, with its long protest against slavery, caste, sectarianism, still lives. It is like the church in Lewis County, feeble and without a pastor. If there is any thing I desire in this world, it is to find some faithful man who will go and minister to that people, and then some faithful men and women who will sustain that man.

In the midst of this season of church planting and church building, there arose a sudden and an unexpected duty; one which speedily involved much perplexity of mind and then anguish of spirit, not to me alone, but to others also; and this not for a day, a week, a month, but, more or less, for years. The relationship once entered upon could not be relinquished without moral delinquency.

The incipient duty was the redemption of a woman, a slave then in my father's family. This woman had lived for years with her husband in the same family and was then the mother of mothers in the same family-the mother of daughters who were mothers. This grandmother, yet comparatively young, was a member of the same church where my father, mother and sister were members. Here, slaves, though members with their masters, were not allowed to sit in the same part of the church house nor at the same time partake of the Lord's Supper with their white fellow Christians. The slaves at this time sat in a gallery at the end of the church house, and when white Christians had been served, one of the elders would say: "Now you black ones, if you wish to commune, come down." This they did by an outside, uncovered rough stairway, and then around outside the house came on to the doors of entrance, and facing the congregation came to the seats vacated for them, and thus ate the Lord's Supper. Thus did slaves indeed "strive to enter into the kingdom of heaven."

Intelligence came to me that my brother had advised my father to sell the woman referred to, for the reason that there were more women in the family than were needed.

I said to my wife: "I cannot redeem all slaves, nor even all in my father's family, but the labors of Julett and her husband contributed in part to the purchase of the land I yet own in Indiana, and to sell those lands and redeem her will be in some measure returning to her and her husband what they have toiled for." My wife said: "Do what you think is right." I took my horse, rode twenty-five miles to my father's house and spent the night. In the morning of the next day I sought an opportunity when my father was alone, and having learned that he would sell, asked what he would take for Julett. He fixed his price. I said: "Will you sell her to me if I bring to you the money?" He said yes. I immediately rode to Germantown and borrowed the requisite amount of money by mortgaging my remaining tract of land for the payment. Whilst there I executed a bill of sale, so that without delay my father could sign it, before he even returned from the field at noon. I tendered to him the money and the bill of sale. He signed the bill of sale, and took the money. I immediately went to "Add," the husband of Julett, and told him I had bought Julett and should immediately secure by law her freedom. I said to him: "I would gladly redeem you but I have not the means." He replied: "I am glad you can free her; I can take care of myself better than she can." I went to the house, wrote a perpetual pass for the woman, gave it to her, and said, "You are a free woman; be in bondage to no man." Tears of gratitude ran down her sable cheeks. I then told her that at the first county-court day I would take her to the clerk's office, where her height could be taken and she be otherwise described, and a record of her freedom made. This was just before the amendment to the State Constitution that forbade emancipation in the State. At noon my father came in and told my mother of the transaction. My mother was displeased,-did not want to spare the woman from certain work for which she was fitted. My father came to me and requested that I

cancel the contract and give up the bill of sale. I said to him, "Here is my horse, and I have a house and lot in Lewis County; I will give them to you if you so desire; but to sell a human being I may not." He became very angry and went to the freed woman and said to her, "When you leave this house never put your foot on my farm again, for I do not intend to have a free nigger on my farm." The woman, the wife and mother, came to me and said, "Master says if I leave here I shall never come back again; I cannot leave my children; I would rather go back into slavery." I said, I have done what I regarded as my duty. To now put you back into slavery, I cannot. We must simply abide the consequences. The woman was in deep distress and helpless as a child. Although I had my horse and was ready to ride, I felt I could not leave the helpless one until a way of relief should open. After a time Julett came to me and said, "As long as mistress shall live I can stand it; I would rather stay." I said, "You are a free woman and must make your own decision. If my father will furnish to you a home, and clothe and feed you, and you shall choose as a free woman to stay, all well; but to sell you back into slavery, I cannot." To this proposition to furnish a home to the freed woman my father agreed. There was now a home for the freed woman, and this with her husband and children and grand-children.

That day of agony was over and eventide had come. I spent the night. The next morning just as I was about starting back to my home, my father said to me, "Julett is here on my premises, and I will sell her before sundown if I can." I turned to him and said, "Father, I am now that woman's only guardian. Her husband cannot protect her,-I only can. I must do as I would be done by; and though it is hard for me to now say to you what I intended to say, yet if you sell that woman, I will prosecute you for so doing, as sure as you are a man." I saw the peril of the defenseless woman. I would gladly have cast from me the cup of a further contest, but I saw that to leave her, though now a free woman, was not the end of obligation. I felt forcibly the applicability of the words, "Cursed be he that doeth the work of the Lord negligently, and cursed be he that keepeth back the sword from blood." Jer. 48: 10. I mounted my horse and rode twelve miles where I could get legal counsel,-counsel on which I could rely. I found that if I left the woman on my father's premises without any public record of her having been sold, the fact of her being then on his premises would be regarded as "prima facie" evidence that she was his property and that he could sell her. I also found that in as much as he had sold her to me, I could, by law, compel him to do that which was just and right,-make a record of the fact of sale. I rode back twelve miles, told my father what was his legal obligation, and asked him to conform to it. He said he would not. I then said to him, "It will be a hard trial for me to arraign my father in a civil court, for neglect of justice to a helpless woman, and also for a plain violation of law; but I will do so, as sure as you are a man, if you do not make the required record of sale." After hesitancy and delay he made the record. These were hours of distress to me, to my father, to my mother, and to the ransomed woman; but the only way to ultimate peace, was to hold on rigidly to the right; though in so doing I had, in the Gospel sense, to leave father, mother, brother, sisters, houses, lands,-all, for Christ's sake. I was conscious that no other motive impelled me.

The legal process ended, the woman was then secure, and in a home, for the time being, with her husband and children. Not long after this my mother died. The services of the freed woman were the more needed where she then was. To her were born, into freedom, three more children. About this time her husband, through a friend, found the record of the time of his bond service. He, by legal process, secured his freedom and recovered several hundred dollars, as compensation for services rendered beyond the time he should have enjoyed his liberty.

After a time the freed woman decided to take her three free children, and go to Ohio, where she could have better opportunities for herself and her little ones. The war of 1861-5 was approaching. Information came to her that my brother, whose home was in New Orleans, La., would, on his return from New York, take all the slave children South. This mother determined to try to save her children from such a fate, and get them, if possible, into freedom. She came to Kentucky to the old home. In the night season she gathered together two sons, three daughters and four grand-children. (Another son had previously been sold, another slave had gone "to parts unknown".) One of these daughters and three grand-children had to be gathered from an adjoining county. Monday morning the mother, with five children and three grandchildren, appeared on the banks of the Ohio river. The sun had already risen and the friends on the other side had gone. The mother, her children and grand-children were captured and put into jail for safe keeping. My father immediately sold all but the freed woman to a slave trader, who shipped all of them to the South. From these we have never heard even a trace.

At the time of this sad occurrence I was eastward, attending a meeting of the A. M. Association. On my way home, and whilst at Cincinnati, Levi Coffin said to me, "John, Julett is in jail, and thy father hath sold all of her children to the slave trader." Instead of going home to my family then out in Madison Co., and, as I had reason to believe they were not in jail, I went up to Bracken County to my father's house. I enquired into the facts. He said, "Yes, I have sold them and have the money in my pocket." I immediately went to see that faithful man, John D. Gregg, and asked him to bail the woman. He agreed to do so. He went to the county judge and offered to be security for the woman's presence at the time for her trial. The judge accepted the offer, and was preparing an obligation for Brother Gregg to sign, when a young attorney came up and served a writ on the woman for stealing slaves (her own child and three grand-children) from another county. The woman was immediately remanded to prison.

My wife was in Bracken County at the time. She went to the prison and asked the privilege of seeing Julett and her children. The wife of the keeper only was there. She told my wife that no one was allowed to go into the jail but the keeper himself. My wife then asked if she could speak to Julett. The wife of the keeper said, "Yes, you can speak through the floor," and turned aside a piece of carpet that covered a crevice in the floor. My wife approached and called. Julett knew her voice and cried out, "Oh, Mis' Tilda; where is Master Gregg?" (Gregg is my middle name; I was known by that name in boyhood days.) My wife said, "He is eastward,-in Massachusetts." Then she cried out, "Oh, Mis' Tilda, what will they do with me?" My wife replied, "They can do no more than send you to the penitentiary; don't be distressed. You have committed no crime; for what mother would not try to get her children out of slavery?" My wife said she could then hear the young mothers and their children crying and sobbing below. My wife again said to Julett, "They can only send you to Frankfort" (the place of the State's prison). "We will come to see you there." By this time white men at the door were cursing, and the jailor's wife was manifestly uneasy. My wife left. As previously stated the children and grand-children were sold and shipped South. The mother had her trial, and was sentenced to the State's prison.

Here, let me say, the torture of the body is terribly cruel, and yet it is the smallest part of the crime of human slavery. I have seen women tied to a tree or a timber and whipped with cow-hides on their bare bodies until their shrieks would seem to rend the very heavens. I have seen a man, a father, guilty only of the crime of absenting himself from work for a day and two nights, on his return home whipped with a cow-hide on his bare flesh until his blood ran to his heels. Thousands of slaves have been whipped and beaten to death even for trivial offenses, as that of a slave in a county adjoining to this, whipped to death for going, in the hour of night, to see his wife, in violation of the master's commands. Yet this torture of the body was the least part of the agony of slavery. The acme of the crime was on the soul. The crushing of human hearts, sundering the ties of husband and wife, parent and child, shrouding all of manhood in the long night of despair,-the crime was on the soul! The agony of our Lord in Gethsemane was that of the soul, not that of the body.

The youth of this generation cannot comprehend the enormity of human slavery,-the effect of it upon society,-how it blunted the sensibilities, outraged every element of justice, fostered licentiousness, violence and crime of almost every description. And yet those who practiced and sustained this iniquity, often occupied commanding positions both in church and state! And here I wish to say, that the same misrepresentation of Christianity is seen in those who maintain the spirit and practice of caste,- a relic of the barbarism of slavery.

To crush by slight or invidious conduct, in church or in civil society, any man or woman of merit, is as truly oppressive and wicked as slavery itself. I speak of conduct toward meritorious persons. As to what our conduct should be we need only to ask what our Lord, our great Exampler, would do were he here in flesh.

Our family visit to Julett Miles, whilst yet in prison, will be given in another chapter.

CHAPTER IV.

Imprisonment of a Colporter.-Assault on Myself.-House Burning.-Church House.-Baptism.-Consideration of the Subject.-Baptism of Myself and Wife.-Invitation to Madison County.-Organization of a Church.-Call to the Church.-Selection of a Place.-Name, Berea.

OTHER scenes of trial awaited us whilst yet in Lewis County. We had colporters in the field who were distributing Bibles, publications of the American Tract Society, and anti-slavery documents. One of these colporters was charged falsely with telling a slave how he might get into a free State. The offense was alleged to have been committed in the adjoining county, and the colporter was therefore arrested and taken to that county and there imprisoned to await his trial. I went to Maysville, Ky., the county seat of that county, that I might minister to the comfort of the prisoner and secure counsel for his defense. On my way home, in a retired place, Thornton H., a violent man, living not far from my home and openly charged with having more children by a slave woman in his kitchen, than by his lawful wife, rushed suddenly upon me, and with a club he had gathered from the woods, struck me across my head, cutting through a Panama hat and leaving a severe bruise. He struck so near his hold on the club that he broke it. Had he struck me on the back of my head he would have killed me. For some unaccountable reason he said not a word, turned his horse suddenly from me, and plunged down a very steep embankment and escaped into a forest. Not long after this, in a re-encounter with another violent man, he was cut across the abdomen, his bowels gushed out, and he died. Thus was the Scripture verified before the people, "the bloody and deceitful man shall not live out half his days." A like fatality followed the men in Bracken, Mason, and Lewis counties, who in like manner had laid violent hands upon me. In common with borne others, I had the conviction that God was my shield.

In the midst of this excitement, the little house used as a school and church house was burned by a poor white man, who was afterward known as a "hired tool." I said to the friends that we must have a larger and a better house in which to worship. The church members were poor, and means small. One young man who afterwards prepared for the ministry, said, "I have not money, but I have two strong hands, and will give fifty days' work toward the erection of the house." My wife said, "Obed, I'll board you." I procured a cross-cut saw, went with neighbors to the woods, cut logs and helped get them to the sawmill, secured contributions, employed carpenters, put on shingles, employed plasterers and made mortar; and it now being winter season, I made and kept up fires until midnight to keep the plastering from freezing. I shared in the work until seats were in the house, and a rough desk was made from which to speak.

Just at this time came a providence which has no small share in shaping the convictions and activities of my life for the past thirty-five years. On one occasion, as I was passing from an appointment in Bracken County to my home then in Lewis County, I called to see Bro. Grundy, the pastor of the Presbyterian church in Maysville. As I was leaving he said to me: "I have a little book I would like to have you read. It is the work of Moses Stuart on Baptism. Stuart," said he, "is, as you know, one of the greatest scholars in America."

I took the book, and rode on ten miles to my home. In my theological course I had not considered the subject of baptism. In my ministry, up to that time, I had been engaged in pressing the claim of the law of love in its application of slave-holding, spirit of caste, secretism and sectism. The church houses built and a measure of quietude secured, I then opened the book and found on page 50 this concession: "In classical use the Greek word *baptizo* means, to dip, plunge or immerse in any liquid; all lexicographers and critics of any note are agreed in this." He then passed to the use of the word in the Septuagint. The Septuagint is the Greek version of the Old Testament. In 2 Kings 5: 14 he rendered *ebaptizeto* by the English word "plunged." "Naaman plunged himself seven times in the Jordan." The propriety of this rendering is seen from the fact that here the verb *baptizo* is the synonym of the Hebrew word *tabal*. To this word Gesenius gives as the only meaning the words "dip", "immerse." I said, If the word means dip, immerse, in the Old Testament, it means the same in the New; for in both the word is used in its religious sense, not merely in its secular sense, but in its religious sense; and in this it means "dip," "immerse." Also the Septuagint version was the version Paul evidently used in his reading of the Scriptures to Greeks in Corinth, in Rome and in all Asia Minor. In addressing a writing to them he would not use the word in a different sense from that in which he read it in the Septuagint. This sense was, as shown by Stuart, the meaning of the word in its classical use, which did not differ from the use of it by the common people. Also let it be noted that to make a revelation to the people, Paul had to use words in the sense in which they were understood by the people. Confessedly in the case of *baptizo* this was "dip," "immerse."

I then passed with Stuart on to his consideration of the word in the New Testament. I saw he accepted "dip" as the proper rendering of *Bapto* as found in Luke 16: 24. In Mark 7:4 he rendered *baptismous* by the, word, washings-admissible only as a resultant meaning;-not a proper meaning when the word is used to designate action; and here we know the pots, to secure the result of washing, cleansing, were dipped. (See Lev. II: 32, Num. 31: 23.) He further added that the word in its figurative use, as in Luke 12: 50, Mark 10: 39, means "overwhelm, and is so used in the classics."

Stuart, in his closing consideration, adds the testimony of the early fathers of the church, as Pastor of Hermas, Justin Martyr and Tertullian; the latter as saying, "There is no difference of consequence between those whom John immersed in the Jordan or Peter in the Tiber"; and then sums all up by saying: "The passages which refer to immersion are so numerous in the fathers that it would take a little volume merely to recite them"; then, closes by a quotation from F. Brenner, a Catholic writer "of learning and ability," as saying that for thirteen hundred years baptism was Generally and ordinarily performed by the immersion of a man under water. This concession, said Stuart, is the more important, from the fact that sprinkling is the present practice of the Roman Catholic church.

After these concessions on the part of Moses Stuart, I took up my Bible and turned to Isa 52: 15; the text so often quoted in favor of sprinkling.

In our version, the rendering is: "So shall he sprinkle many nations." I saw from the connection that the passage had no reference to the Gospel ordinance, and that the word translated sprinkle, as I have shown in my book on Christian Baptism, when applied to mind, as there used, cannot mean scatter in particles, but refers to the joys of salvation through Christ, as there referred to. Literally rendered, it reads, "So shall he cause many nations to leap for joy." The context demands such a rendering. (See Gesenius, word, *Naza.*) I then turned to Ezek. 36: 25. I saw that this text also had no reference to the ordinance of baptism under the Gospel dispensation, but to the moral purification of the Jews when they should be gathered from the heathen nations. Let the reader study the connection. The water of "separation" or of purification as designated in the Hebrew text is not *mayim hayim*, pure water, but *mayim tahorim*, water of purification,-a fluid made of the ashes of a red heifer and pure water. Barnes, in his comment on this passage, says: "The practice of sprinkling with consecrated water is referred to as synonymous with purifying,"-moral purification.

The sprinkling of the water of "separation" was a part of the process of ceremonial cleansing; (see Num. 19: 19)-here used figuratively-"synonymous with purifying." "From all your idols will I cleanse you,"-you Jews. There is here no reference whatever to Christian baptism. In my personal review, I passed to the New Testament,-saw that John baptized the people, not *with* the river Jordan, but in the river Jordan (Mark 1: 5); and that our Lord, as stated in the ninth verse, was baptized-literally "plunged into the Jordan,"-that as recorded in Acts 8: 38, 39, Philip and the eunuch went down into the water and Philip baptized him, and they came up out of the water. I passed to Rom. 6: 3, 4, where Paul represented believers as having been baptized into death, i.e., into the relation of dead ones, and therefore properly, by symbol, buried with Christ by baptism into this relation of dead ones-that as the bread and wine set forth the body and blood of our Lord, so the burial and resurrection of believers in their baptism set forth, not only their spiritual death to sin and resurrection to newness of life, but also the burial and resurrection of our Lord.

I noticed the uniform concessions of such authorities as Tholuck, Lange, Whitby, Macknight, Clarke and others that the word baptizo means immerse; that Calvin himself said, "The word baptize means immerse entirely; and it is certain that the custom of thus entirely immersing was anciently observed in the church"; but he then assumes the papal dogma, "that the church has reserved to herself the right to change the form somewhat, retaining the substance." I saw, what is true, that no man, and no set of men, have a right to change a positive command, an ordinance of divine appointment. To do so is fearful sacrilege: also in changing the form of a symbol we lose the truth thus symbolized. This is treachery though good men and women see it not. I saw something of my responsibility as a preacher of the Gospel-that it behooved me to get all the light I could on this divinely appointed ordinance. Dr. Edward Beecher had published a book which among pedo-baptists, was held in high repute. I ordered the book and read his argument about "purifying." I said, His mistake is that he takes the import of the rite for the meaning of the word, when used to designate the action of the rite. To illustrate,-the import of the rite of sprinkling is that of cleansing, as "hearts sprinkled, cleansed, from an evil conscience." But the meaning of the word when used to designate action means not to purify, but to scatter in particles; so the word baptize, when used to designate action, means immerse-not purify-which is the import of the rite itself.

I saw many preachers do as Dr. Edward Beecher, baptize their fingers in water, then sprinkle a few drops on the head of the penitent (*rhantize*);-and then call this totally different act baptism; saying, "The thing to be done is to symbolize purification." I said if that had been the thing commanded, then the penitent might have been "passed through the fire"; for such was a symbol of purification. But God commanded a specific thing, "Go baptize, immerse"; and the connection shows that the immersion was in water; and this not merely for the purpose of symbolizing purification, but also other important facts; as our own spiritual death to sin and resurrection to "newness of life," the burial and resurrection of our Lord (Rom. 6: 4), and our own resurrection (1 Cor. 15:29.) I said, Sprinkling cannot emblematize these important facts.

Other good men say the word means "wash"; and accordingly baptize their hands in water and take up enough to effect a local washing on the head; then assume that such a transaction is the fulfillment of the command, "Go baptize them,"-the person,-the entire man.

We may here properly notice that wash is a resultant meaning; as wet is a resultant meaning of sprinkle, though not the meaning of the word when used to designate action. When used to designate action, the word sprinkle means scatter in particles. So wash is not the proper meaning of the word baptize, when used to designate action. Then the word as applied to men means "dip," immerse (see 2 Kings 5: 14). The word here translated dip, immerse, is the same word which our Lord used when he said, "Go disciple all nations Baptizonites]-baptizing them." And if the word in 2 Kings 5:14 means immerse, then as found in Matt. 28:19, it means immerse. Also if immersion is baptism, which all admit as true, then a totally different act, like sprinkling or pouring, is not. I also saw that in positive commands as "eat," "drink," "circumcise," "baptize," we must have specific words indicating specific actions, or we would not know what to do-we would be without a revelation,-in this matter. I saw that this following or resultant meaning was the source of much of the confusion among the sects.

I also saw some were following the traditions and opinions of men. Others were following their feelings,-considering what would be most pleasant to themselves. Others were following their own reasoning to what would be sufficient. I said, All this is going in the "way of Cain": and cannot be pleasing to God. I must do the thing he commands.

I told my wife my convictions,-that I believed our Lord was immersed, and that his commission was that disciples be baptized, immersed, in his name. She replied: "I have been feeling so for two years." We had both been consecrated to the Lord by sprinkling-rhantism-but not by baptism. By this time "baptism" by sprinkling was to me as much a solecism as immersion by aspersion. We decided to live up to our convictions of duty and be baptized. But the question arose, whom shall we ask to baptize us? We did not know a minister in the State who would at that time be willing to baptize us, nor did we know one, with his practice of, or conservative notions about, slavery by whom we would be willing to be baptized.

Through Wm. Goodell I had learned something of the history of Francis Hawley, a native of North Carolina, and who, whilst there, maintained, as a Baptist minister, a strong protest against human slavery, and was at that time ministering to undenominational churches near to Syracuse, New York. I wrote to him and requested that he come to Kentucky and baptize me and my wife. He came; and near to our little cottage, and in the presence of our dear children and a large concourse of people, he buried us by baptism in the waters of Cabin Creek, Lewis Co., Ky.

By that transaction we said to our children and to our neighbors, we believe Christ our Lord was buried, that he rose again, and that we in like manner will rise again and walk with him in glorified form.

As opportunity allowed, I studied the subject of baptism still more fully. I saw clearly that the ordinance of baptism was designed to emblematize great facts in the Gospel; like the burial and resurrection of our Lord, which sprinkling could not do,-that the truths thus set forth needed to be presented in a brief manner to young and old. Accordingly I prepared matter for a small book, on the topic of Christian Baptism, Action and Subjects, and published it.

As a justification for this form of labor let me say, that whilst my life has been devoted to the maintenance of the fundamental principles of Christianity, love to God and love to man; and whilst I insist upon the fact that the inner, the spiritual is the vital feature of Christianity, I do not forget that the external rites of Christianity are important. They not only symbolize the internal, but the observance of them is also a demonstration to the outside world, but is that which actualizes to the

I have baptized all of my children, save Tappan, who died when in his third year. I baptized my eldest son Burritt, when he was seven years old. At five he would read the Scriptures and pray with the family. He knew what trust in Christ was and the symbolic import of his burial in baptism. The four other children I baptized on profession of their faith in Christ; with this coincidence: each one at the time of his or her baptism was between the years of ten and eleven. Early in life children may be trained,- trained to love and serve the Lord.

As opportunity allowed, I studied the subject of baptism still more fully. I saw that the ordinance of baptism was designed to emblematize great facts in the Gospel, like the burial and resurrection of our Lord, which sprinkling could not do; that the truths thus set forth needed to be presented in a brief manner to young and old. Accordingly I prepared matter for a small book, on the subject of Christian Baptism,-Action and Subjects, and published the book.

I never sprinkle, because I believe our Lord in his great commission commanded me to do something else,-baptize, not sprinkle. I say to believers, Study God's Word; live up to your convictions; I must live up to mine. I recognize the fact that our word baptize is not a translation, but simply the Greek word transferred with an English termination affixed and must therefore be interpreted by the reader of English. True believers may differ in the interpretation. I feel that as a true Protestant and Christian, I must grant to a true believer the right of "private interpretation." I therefore fellowship in church relationship those who manifest true faith in Christ as their Saviour from sin, though they may make a mistake in the action they design as baptism. The mistake in the act of consecration does not destroy Christian character. Our Lord prayed for the union of all true believers (John 17:21). We can be united on Christ: on opinions we cannot. We may expect that with human creeds and sects out of the way, men and women, delivered from the bias of party teaching, will, in the light of other parallel passages, come to see the truth alike in reference to this rite of divine appointment, and as in apostolic times, there will yet be "One Lord, one faith, one baptism"-not that several different acts were regarded as baptism, but that to Gentiles as well as to Jews, one and the same rite was applied; and that, as I believe, not a rhantism, but a baptism.

Prior to my baptism, Mr. C. M. Clay had returned from Mexico and had requested that I send to his care a box of my "Anti-slavery Manuals." I had done so. He distributed these largely in this part of Madison County. Friends of freedom here had united in a request that I visit them and preach to them. I did so early in the spring of 1853. After I had preached to the people some nine sermons, thirteen persons came out as professed followers of Christ. Most of these had been baptized and came from their former slaveholding fellowships. The others were baptized, and all united as a church and for a time worshiped in the old Glade meeting house. After some days, I left the little flock and returned to my home in Lewis County.

In the new church was a brother who, in capacity to speak, was an Apollos. The church invited him to preach to them. After some months, brethren in the church wrote that their pastor was not doing well, and entreated that I come to their help or the church would be scattered, lost. I saw that if this church, planted as it was in the interior of the State and avowedly on the principle that Christ is no respecter of persons, and is not the minister of sin in any form, should now be allowed to fail, such failure would be a calamity. I said to my wife, For us now to leave these churches on the border of the State, just at the time when they are springing up into a measure of prosperity and efficiency,-to sell out our small effects, take our little ones and go 140 miles into the interior and into a place comparatively a wilderness, without schools, railroads, or even turnpikes, will be a privation, to say the least. But I said, My mission is to preach the gospel of love in Kentucky. To go to the interior would enlarge my sphere of labor, and apparently increase my power at home and abroad. I said, I have no right to please myself at the expense of the interests of Christ's kingdom. My wife said, "If you feel that it is duty so to do, we will go, and leave the future with God."

Just at this time a Bro. J. S. Davis, a native of Virginia, a graduate from Galesburg, Ill., afterward from the theological school at Oberlin, Ohio, expressed a desire to enter into the work in Kentucky. The churches on the border accepted his labors, and thus the way was made clear for me to go into the interior.

I sent forward an appointment, and then took my horse and rode to the interior and engaged in preaching for a few days. Mr. C. M. Clay had bought a tract of land containing some 600 acres; the tract included most of the ground on which the village of Berea now stands. Mr. Clay was very desirous that the church should be sustained, and offered to give to me a farm out of the 600 acres if I would come and become the settled pastor. I never made a bargain with any man or people to come for a price, but always decided first where duty called and then took what, in the providence of God, should come. So I did in this case. During the meeting, our mutual friend, H. Rawlings, came to me and said: "Clay wants you to go and select a farm as a home." Though I had decided in my own mind I would come, and would need a place as a home, yet I said to Rawlings, "I will not go and select, for in so doing I may spoil the sale of a lot for Mr. Clay; and especially I will not divert my mind with anything until this meeting is over." Rawlings said: "The surveyor is here." I said, "Then you go and mark me off a spot." He and Bro. W. B. Wright came to the extreme corner of the 600 acre tract and surveyed off for me ten acres of land.

When the meeting had ended, I took my horse and rode to the place selected, the selection of which I had left to the guidance of providence, rather than leave what I then thought to be the post of duty. When I came to the place I found about one acre of hillside, half cleared, and the rest of the land covered with a dense undergrowth of "blackjacks" and a frog pond in the midst. A human habitation could not be seen from the place. I got on my horse and rode back to the place where Mr. Clay then was and said to him, "The lot selected by our friends is a dreary spot to which to bring a family, and is more than a mile from the place where we propose to build a church house." Mr. Clay quickly asked, "Is there any other spot to you more desirable?" I said, "The Maupin House is near to the site for the proposed church house, and more desirable."

He replied: "I have just sold that to Dave Kinnard", and standing there as he was by Kinnard's shop, he cried out: "Dave, come out here; what will you take for your house and lot I sold to you?"

Kinnard asked, "What do you want it for?" Mr. Clay replied, "For the preacher." Said Kinnard, "He may have it." I knew Kinnard was a "trading" man, and whether he designed the property as a home or for speculation, I knew not. I said to him, "Come aside"; and then asked, "Why did you buy that piece of property?" He had another property alongside of it. He replied, "It is my 'rosy'." I saw in a moment that to take the house and lot would be to covet my neighbor's property. I said at once, "I will not take it." I rode back to the selected spot. There I found the two friends, H. Rawlings and W. Stapp, sitting each on an old fallen tree. I said, "This is a dreary spot to which to bring a family." All was silence for a moment. Rawlings, who was not a Christian, then broke the silence by quoting the familiar couplet:

"Prisons would palaces prove,
If Jesus would dwell with me there."

I said to Stanton Thompson, who had that moment come up, seeking employment, "Take your axe and drive a stake by that little hickory, and we will build a house there."

Looking around for a moment I saw, what I had not previously noticed, the absence of water, and said, "There is no water here for man or beast." Silence again for a moment, when Rawlings gravely replied, "Moses smote the rock and the waters gushed out." I said to Thompson, "Dig a well beside that dogwood tree." He did,-found water,-and the well has never been dry.

CHAPTER V.

Removal to Madison County.-Projected College. Its Foundation Principles.-Survey of Fields.-Mob at Dripping Springs.-Mob in Rockcastle County.- Fourth of July.-C. M. Clay and I differ.-Mob in Rockcastle County.-Mob in Madison County.-Dark Days at Berea.-Entreaty to Leave.-Decision to Hold On.-Trusts.

I RETURNED to my family then in Lewis County. After a short time, I gathered our household goods into a two-horse wagon, and my wife, two children and I, in a one-horse carriage, started for the new home, one hundred and forty miles in the interior. There was no railroad to Berea at that time. In the evening of the third day we camped in the new house, then without a chimney, or glass in the windows, or fence around the yard. Believing, as we did, that we were exactly where the Lord would have us, we lay down and slept calmly, sweetly.

After a few days, with chimney up, glass in the windows, and yard enclosed, we began to plan for a school-house, and a place for preaching up on the ridge. Lumber was secured and the eastern part of what is now known as the "old District School-house" was constructed.

About this time Bro. George Candee came; and whilst he and I were chopping wood, then piled up in my yard, we talked up the idea of a more extended school-a college-in which to educate not merely in a knowledge of the sciences, so called, but also in the principles of love in religion, and liberty and justice in government; and thus permeate the minds of the youth with these sentiments.

With a purpose to survey the field and look out the best location, we took our horses and rode out into Rockcastle County, and visited a community in which I had preached a few discourses during the preceding year. We thought we had there found the place, and unfolded our plans to a friend. He entered with commendable zeal into the plan and was ready to deed lands for the enterprise.

As a preparatory step we induced friends to help in the erection of a house as a place for the school, and for public worship. The building was speedily enclosed, a few sermons preached, and Otis B. Waters, a student from Oberlin, Ohio, was introduced as teacher of the school. Soon some enemy of the movement reduced the building to ashes.

Friends there were intimidated and wholly unwilling to make any other effort at building. I kept up a monthly appointment in the community, in groves and private houses.

Brother Candee went into Pulaski County and started a school there. Speedily the house there was burned. From thence he went to McKee, the county seat of Jackson County. I kept headquarters at Berea, with regular appointments there, and in three other adjoining counties.

A Bro. Richardson, a man of excellent spirit, came. He went on to Williamsburg, the county seat of Whitley County, where Bro. Myers has successfully labored. Bro. Richardson there began a school, but soon felt the unfriendly embrace of a mob and left.

One of my appointments for regular preaching, at this time, was at Dripping Springs, in Garrard County, near to Crab Orchard. The slave power was, as ever, vigilant-called a meeting of citizens at Crab Orchard, and a venerable minister of the Gospel (?) presided over their deliberations. They gravely resolved that I should not further preach nor distribute Abolition documents in that county.

On coming to my next appointment, I found, as I had been told I would, a crowd not very benignant in looks. I went into the house with friendly salutations for all, and with quiet purpose to meet faithfully whatever providence might reveal. I was informed that there was, in the hands of Dr. _____, a batch of resolutions I would be requested to hear. I expressed a readiness to listen. At the close of the reading the demand was that my reply be yes or no. I said, "I have given to you a quiet, respectful hearing, and have a right to the same from you"; and without pause for them to accumulate wrath replied to each resolution-six in number.

In my reply I said: "I am a citizen, a native of the State; my interests are your interests; your interests are my interests; and as a servant of the living God, and deprecating, as I do, the institution of slavery in all its forms, I cannot pledge to you that I will not preach in this county what I conceive to be the truth of God, or refrain from scattering abroad tracts and other publications containing sentiments of justice and liberty." A significant pause ensued. The crowd sought, through a "go-between," to pile up the sad consequences that might follow if I did not then quietly withdraw. I replied, "You all know I am not a man of violence,-I carry no weapons of defense. If any person is hurt, the guilt and responsibility will be on those who do the 'hurting.'" After much counciling and hesitancy, one swore he could move me; another swore he could-and another-and the three clamped me; and with the crowd pressing they soon hustled me from the house. As they were passing with me out of the yard, I laid hold of a bar-post, deciding as I did, in my mind, that if they got me away it should be a case of "assault and battery." This they soon made, by breaking my hold. They took me to my horse, which they had brought from the stable, and asked me to get on. I declined, saying: "I can not, with any degree of propriety, comply with demands so unreasonable, unjust and illegal." They then put me on my horse and asked me to ride; I declined. They then led and drove, and thus escorted me one or two miles on my way home.

I made my appeal, as I had done in similar cases before, to the Civil Court. I got no redress. When my friend Rawlings enquired of the foremen of the Grand Jury why they did not bring in a true bill against the mob, the foreman replied, "The proof was clear, but we could not do any thing."

Other trials, by which to sift friends, and indicate the place for the proposed college and continued church, seemed to be necessary.

Soon after the mobbing at Dripping Springs, Garrard County, I went again eighteen miles distant, to my regular monthly appointment in Rockcastle County. My wife taking her babe in her arms, leaving our other little ones at home with a good friend, went with me. When we arrived, we found an orderly congregation of people, and larger than we had expected, assembled in the grove, according to previous arrangement.

Soon after I had commenced preaching, a band of men, about thirty in number, rode up, dismounted and posted themselves outside the congregation. Soon it was manifest that they were in doubt as to what was the better course to pursue. Unobserved by me, and without any previous knowledge of his intent, there stood behind me a strong, robust man; and, though it was now early summer, he had on a large overcoat, with large side pockets, evidently not empty. Under his overcoat, as I was afterward informed, there was seen the handle of a huge knife, evidently not made by Wostenholm & Sons. This man (Roberts) said not a word, nor moved a step. His known sympathy with liberty and free speech, bespoke to others his silent purpose. I followed the plan of my sermon, concluded, and knelt down, with many others, and called on a brother to lead in prayer-he was silent. I then called on a venerable minister of the Gospel, usually fervent in prayer, and he, too, remained silent. I prayed, and then, after further conversation with some three persons who had confessed sorrow for sin and trust in Jesus, we went with the congregation to a stream of water near by, and there, upon the repeated profession of their faith in Christ, I baptized the three, in the name of the Father, Son, and Holy Spirit.

Soon after the baptism and before we left the ground, my wife, other friends and myself, were warned not to return-that if we did, we would certainly meet a large force, and I not be allowed to speak. I replied, "The Lord willing, I will meet my appointment." My wife told them that, if living, I would come.

In the meantime, I went in person to see two civil officers-justices of the peace. They were personal friends. Each promised to attend the next meeting and demand order in the name of the Commonwealth.

I sought at all times to secure to myself and to others protection of person and liberty of speech, by appeal, not to arms, but to civil magistrates and to civil courts. This was, as I believed, not only wise policy, but religious duty. Civil authority is from God. "The powers that be are ordained of God." Rom. 13:1. Parental authority is of God. It may be, and often is, abused. So may civil authority; still it is right to recognize and honor the civil authority, thus educate public sentiment to a right course, and secure in this way the only substantial peace.

My appeals to the magistrates referred to, though they were personally friendly, were of no avail.

Between the meeting referred to and my next appointment in Rockcastle County, there came a severe crisis in the history of the work at Berea and the region roundabout.

A short time previous in that year, 1856, Hon. C. M. Clay had proposed a Republican ticket for Kentucky; a convention in which it might be adopted and sent forth. In his introductory speech he said: "The National Government has nothing more to do with slavery than with concubinage in Turkey." I, in reply, said, "The National Government is responsible for the strength and perpetuity of slavery and this by the enactment of the Fugitive Slave Law."

The Fourth of July was near at hand. We had previously, on this national birthday, celebrated liberty prospectively-Mr. Clay leading and I following.

The place for the celebration had, by previous arrangements, been fixed at Slate Lick Springs, Madison County. The day came, and hundreds of people gathered. Mr. Clay and I were on hand, and when the hour for addresses came, Mr. Clay said that I must speak first. I declined. He insisted. I thought I saw his policy-have me utter my radical sentiments, and he then review me.

I decided, in my own mind, to meet the issue squarely; and rising with a copy of the Declaration of Independence in my hand, I repeated the words, " 'All men are created free and equal,' and 'endowed by their Creator with certain inalienable rights.' " I said, "If inalienable, then such are man's relations to God, to himself and family, that he cannot alienate; society cannot; governments cannot alienate. 'Endowed by their Creator,' if so, then it is impious in us to attempt to take away." I added, "This invasion of human rights is condemned by the highest judicial authorities"; and I quoted from Blackstone, Judge McLean, and others. Then I said, "What is stronger than all, the Word of God forbids it," and quoted various passages. I further said, "That which thus outrages natural right and divine teaching is mere usurpation, and, correctly speaking, is incapable of legalization." I then showed that under the Mansfield decision there was no legal slavery in any of the British colonies-that when the American colonies became States of this Union, they did not attempt to legalize slavery-it exists only by usurpation. I then concluded by saying, "A law confessedly contrary to the law of God ought not by human courts to be enforced"; and referred to the Fugitive Slave Law, and said that I would refuse to obey; then suffer the penalty.

Mr. Clay followed, and after expressions of high personal regard for me, in many respects, he said to others, "As my political friends, I warn you; Mr. Fee's position is revolutionary, insurrectionary and dangerous." He continued by saying, "As long as a law is on the statute book, it is to be respected and obeyed until repealed by the republican majority." He elaborated his position. When he came to the Fugitive Slave Law he said, "So far as this is concerned, I would not obey it myself; it is contrary to natural right, and I would not degrade my nature by obeying it,"-a manly, noble utterance. I seized the concession and the opportunity and in my reply said, "My friend, Mr. Clay, has conceded the whole point at issue-that there is a Higher Law." He, now seated in the midst of the congregation, cried out, "The Fugitive Slave Law is unconstitutional." Yet it was on the statute book and unrepealed by the republican majority; and to be logically in harmony with his previous premises, he would be under obligation to enforce and carry it out. There was manifest confusion in the crowd. A slaveholder standing by W. B. Waight said, "Fee has got him." The slaveholder was sorry that it was so. I refer to this simply to show that even slaveholders saw the absolute right; but, with many others, were unwilling to stand up for the right.

The provisions in the baskets were spread, but eaten without exhilaration. The friends of slavery were not pleased, and the friends of freedom were divided. Some went away saying, "Fee is religiously right; Clay is politically right."

Many whose consciences were in favor of freedom, but who had not yet counted all but loss for Christ in the person of his poor, fell back, one by one.

Mr. Clay himself came not to my house for thirteen months; and when the time came for me to go back to my next appointment in Rockcastle County, not only were the magistrates, alluded to previously, secure at home, but many others also remained. The prospect for a college, a living church, life itself, was waning. The "narrow way" still existed.

Soon after the celebration at Slate Lick, the time for my next appointment in Rockcastle County came. That the now drooping spirits of remaining friends might be cheered by my personal presence, and that all things might be in readiness for worship on Lord's Day, I mounted my horse the day previous, and rode out, some eighteen miles, to the place appointed for preaching. On my way I called at the house of one of the magistrates previously referred to. He could not be found. I then rode on to the house of the man who had been apparently most interested in our work. I saw in a moment that he, too, was utterly discouraged,-no spirit in him-afraid to go to the place appointed for preaching, though on his own premises. He was willing to shelter me for the night,-but that was all.

Then next morning the heavens themselves were overcast with clouds; and about the time for the gathering of the people, the rain commenced descending. The house provided for the expected congregation was small and soon filled, almost exclusively with women. The arbor, constructed as a shade for men, in front of the house, would not shield them from the falling rain. They dispersed to neighboring houses. This was the opportunity for the mob foretold at the time of the previous appointment.

As I was afterward informed, the mob was at this time lying in ambush, waiting to see if Mr. Clay and his personal friends would be present. They knew that immediately after the mob at Dripping Springs Mr. Clay had said, "Free speech shall be maintained, and Fee shall be heard"; and strong demonstrations for the maintenance of such had been made; but these men also knew that since that time Mr. Clay, as at the celebration at Slate Lick, had expressed disapproval of my radical sentiments in regard to the Higher Law. They were now waiting to see if Mr. Clay's difference of sentiment would neutralize his zeal for free speech, and cause his absence on this occasion. Finding him not present, and no armed forces ready to defend me, some forty or fifty men quickly surrounded the house in which I was preaching; and a portion of them, with show of previously-concealed weapons, rushed into the house, and with violence pulled me out of it, tearing my coat, and one man struck me a violent blow, but without inflicting lasting injury.

The mob had taken the precaution to have my horse in readiness, and demanded that I mount and be ready to march. I saw that this, under existing circumstances, was probably the best thing to do.

The leader of the mob said to me, "We will now take you out of this county; and if you return again it will be at the peril of your life." I calmly replied, "I am in your hands, but I will make no pledges to men, for the present or the future." The crowd started with me for Crab Orchard, nine miles distant.

The men having me in charge were not silent. Like all others conscious of guilt, they sought to justify themselves by criminating others. I was neither sullen nor silent. I vindicated my right as a native citizen, and as a Christian minister, to speak as occasion offered, and appealed to their own sense of honor and of right. One by one of the number dropped out of the crowd.

We had not proceeded many miles until suddenly there descended upon us a drenching rain;-like the dew on Nebuchadnezzar: as described by Milton, it "dipped us all over." By common consent we all took shelter in a farm house near to the roadside. The "man of the house" had a kind look and a pleasant manner. Seeing a large Bible on a small table, I said to him, "We can not travel whilst the rain is falling so heavily, and if you are willing we will read a portion of Scripture and pray." He assented pleasantly, and I turned to the fifty-eighth chapter of Isaiah, and read, "Cry aloud, spare not, lift up thy voice like a trumpet, * * * Is not this the fast that I have chosen? to loose the bands of wickedness, to undo the heavy burdens, and to let the oppressed go free, and that ye break every yoke? * * Then shalt thou call and the Lord shall answer";-and so to the end of that chapter, so full of instruction and precious promise. I knelt down and prayed. Soon the rain ceased. We all mounted our horses; but seven of the number turned back. Nine persevered in their purpose to take me out of the county, and brought me to Crab Orchard, where, much to my comfort, I saw no crowd of hostile men waiting to receive me, as was expected.

The mission of the nine to take me out of the county was now ended; but feeling that they must say something they asked me if I would "take something to drink,"-they meant whisky.

These men, as their manner indicated, doubtless thought they were acting magnanimously to offer a "treat"-even to an Abolitionist. I, in a quiet manner, replied, "I drink nothing stronger than cold water; and if you will give me a cup of that I shall be much obliged." This they quickly brought to me, and after drinking it, I bade them good evening and started toward my home.

It was now near sunset. I rode on some two or three miles, and coming to the small log-house of a poor man, I asked the privilege of spending with him the night. This he kindly granted. Early the next morning I was again on my horse, and in a few minutes was in the well known road leading from Dripping Springs to Berea.

During the night a friend, James Waters, came across the country, and came to my house exactly as the clock was striking twelve. My wife recognized his voice and said, "Mr. Fee is taken"; for all night long she seemed to have had an apprehension of my condition. Waters, after some minutes of delay, said, with a tremulous voice, "He is in the hands of a violent mob, and where they have gone with him God only knows."

Our dear Burritt, now gone before us, then a boy seven years old, said, "Mother, we can all pray for Pa." The mother and children, with Miss Tucker, a lady friend from Oberlin, Ohio, all knelt down and offered earnest prayer.

Soon, Mrs. W. B. Wright, the wife of our nearest neighbor, was at the door of our house, and promptly offered to go with my wife in search of me; and by dawn of day, twenty-two men were ready to go with the women.

Waters, who knew the character of the men who had seized me, had expressed the belief that I would not be found alive.

In less than three hours the company was near to the place where I had been last seen in the hands of the mob. Just at this moment a friend rode up and informed them that I had been seen that morning riding quietly toward my home. All quickly retraced their steps, and soon found me quite happy with the little ones, who had been left in the care of Miss Tucker. Thus ended another episode in the history of Berea and its work.

It was now manifest that the place for the contemplated college was not in Rockcastle County; at least in that part of it. The women of true faith in God were few there; and the men of courage were still less in number.

Providence seemed to say, fall back on Berea; and though there were then few in Berea with depth of piety, there were others who had physical courage, and who believed that free speech is right and had determined it should be maintained. Thus "the earth helped the woman"-for a time.

Other trials were in reserve, by which to test the faith and patience of the church and people at Berea. In the years 1857-8 I had appointments for preaching at Lewis Chapel in this county, in the region known as Big Bend of Kentucky River. In this region Bro. Robert Jones had also traveled as a colporter, selling the publications of the American Tract Society, and also distributing anti-slavery documents,-tracts written by myself and others.

In the month of February, 1858, I went to the house of a Mr. Fields, an excellent man, a substantial farmer; and on Friday evening preached at his house.

I had been warned not to come again into that region; but my covenant was upon me to preach the Gospel of Christ in this my native State-a gospel that is not the minister of sin;-and there was thus far an open door, and I

MRS. MATILDA H. FEE.

Mrs. Matilda H. Fee felt, as ofttimes before, "woe is me if I preach not this Gospel"; and that I had no right to "count my life dear unto myself."

Saturday morning was one of comparative comfort for that month of the year. After breakfast I retired to an adjacent forest for prayer and reflection. On returning to the house, Mr. Fields said to me, "Mr. C_____, ex-member of the Legislature, has been here, and advises me not to go to the chapel; 'for,' said he, 'There will be trouble to-day.'"

Just at this moment a man rode by carrying before him three double-barreled shotguns. "There," said Mr. Fields, "do you see that half-Injun? He lives at C_____ O_____'s: there is something up." Turning to me and looking gravely he said, "Shall we take guns? I have one rifle, and my brother has two." I replied, "No, I carry no weapons but the gospel of truth; and then, three rifles will only provoke greater violence. If we shall be disturbed I will make my appeal to the Civil Courts, as I always have done." He assented. In due season we took our horses and started for the chapel,-the place for preaching.

When we arrived, Mr. Marsh, a friend, who was outside waiting for us, advancing, said, in a very subdued tone, "We shall have trouble here to-day." I replied, "Let us do our duty, and leave the results with God"; and passed on into the house; for when duty is clear, it is not wise to counsel with fears. Mr. Marsh followed in, and seated himself near to the desk where I stood. He seemed to desire to be near to me. Exactly on time, eleven o'clock, we commenced the service of the morning. I had advanced about half way in my sermon, when I noticed restiveness in the congregation, and some young men left the house. I knew the occasion, for I was so situated that I, too, could see the crowds of men, on horseback, with guns on their shoulders, riding rapidly toward the chapel.

In a moment the house was surrounded with armed men. I said to the congregation, "Sit still"; and I preached on. Soon Mr. C____ came in, and seated himself by Mr. Marsh. C_____ commenced whispering to Marsh. Marsh shook his head, and C_____ got up and retired from the house. I continued preaching as though all was right. Soon C_____ came in, and advancing to me said, "Mr. Fee, there are men here who want you to stop and come out." I said, "Mr. Covington, I am engaged in a religious duty and in the exercise of a constitutional right; please sit down and do not interrupt." He turned on his heel, and went out. Soon three men entered the doorway, with guns in their hands, and with horrible oaths cried out, "Stop, G-d d-n you, and come out here." I preached on. Marsh, Fields, and others-men and women-remained, still apparently listening. Soon the men referred to rushed forward, and seizing me by the collar of my coat, and by my arms, dragged me to the door. There a stout man, S_____, stepped up, and pulling a new rope from his pocket, swore he would "hang me to the first limb, if I did not then promise to leave the county and never come back again." I replied, "I am in your hands, men; you know I would not harm one of you; if you harm me, upon you will be the responsibility." With violence they pulled me out into the highway,-the county road.

The captain of the company, coming up, said, "I am captain of this company; leave him in my hands." They surrendered. The captain led me aside, and with the concurring entreaty of Mr. C____, advised me to promise these men that I would leave the county and not come back again; assuring me if I would do so they would not hurt me. I replied, "I am not hasty in this my purpose to preach this gospel of impartial love, and bear my testimony against this great perversion of it, human slavery. I cannot pledge myself to leave where I believe duty calls."

They then brought my horse and demanded that I mount. I did so. They then went back into the chapel and brought out Bro. Jones; and the captain of the company took him behind him on his horse, and they started with us for Kentucky River, distant, perhaps, two miles, swearing they would duck me as long as life was in me. The ducking I dreaded, for the weather was cool,-in February-the river at full tide, and I not an expert swimmer. Soon after starting, the captain, addressing himself to me, commenced talking obscenely. I turned to him and asked if he had a mother.-He replied, "Yes." I then asked, "Have you a wife?" He again replied, "Yes." I said, "I hope, out of respect to your mother and your wife, if not to others, you will speak as a son and husband ought to." He was silent for a time. Slavery was a corrupt tree, and bore corrupt fruit,-made many of those who consented to it, not only lawless, but lecherous and vile. Faithful men and women needed to cry out against it.

When the crowd had advanced about half the distance to the river, the captain called a halt, and again demanded that I promise to leave the county and not return again; and added, "You have said that the men engaged in mobs are generally poor and irresponsible men; but we will have you understand that the men in this crowd are men of property and standing." I replied, "So much the greater peril to society, when men of property and standing will consent to disregard law and order." I again said, "I can make no pledges to leave." They then started again for the river.

I had been in the hands of several organized mobs before. I had been in the midst of infuriated crowds not organized, who seemed ready to rush upon me, but were in some way hindered. I had been often waylaid and suddenly assaulted. I had been stoned on the highway; but this was the most formidable of all, and, apparently, "meant business." The mob took us near to the bank of the river. There the leaders left me in the care of others, and turned off to counsel with men who were for some reason already on the ground.

The men left to guard me were manifestly poor men, with some young men. These seemed to enter into sympathy with me, and in an undertone one said to me, "Just promise these men to leave, and they will not hurt you." I replied, "It is not fitting that I, a native citizen, pledge to these men that I leave my home and the work to which I believe God has called me." I said, "You cannot see my motives now; you will at the Judgment Day." By this time the leaders had returned, and men were around me in circles three deep, and heard these last words. One cried out, "We did not come here to hear a sermon, let us do our work." They then took Bro. Jones and myself nearer to the bank of the river and ordered Bro. Jones to strip himself. He took off his coat. The captain cried out, "Take off your jacket." He did so. "Now your shirt-strip to the red." Jones hesitated. The captain stripped him to the bare back, bent the man down, and with three sycamore rods, heavy and thick, struck the unoffending man many severe blows, leaving the marks on his body as distinct as the fingers on a man's hand. The suffering man groaned and fell forward.

The captain then turned to me, and, with an oath, said, "I will give you five hundred times as much if you do not promise to leave this county and not come back again." I said to him, "I will take my suffering first," and knelt down. One of the crowd, whom I then knew not-who "held the clothes"-now an official in the county, and a very estimable citizen, cried out, "Don't strike him." Then another cried out, "Don't strike him." O____ said, "I feel that I ought to, but don't like to go against my party;-get up and go home."

I got on my horse, and took Bro. Jones behind me, for he was so disabled by the whiping that he could not walk.

The retreat of these men of "property and standing," from their work at the Big Bend of Kentucky River, was ludicrously orderly. The captain ordered all to march away in double file. The column was quite long and imposing. Bro. Jones and I, two unarmed men on one horse, in the middle, the men of "property" in front, and the men of "standing" in the rear.

The procession marched in this manner for some two or three miles. On coming to Covington's factory, the command was given, "Right about, wheel." This was meant for those who had enlisted for the previously described "service." Bro. Jones and I had not thus enlisted; hence we kept the straightforward road, as all then desired us to do.

After a ride of one or two miles, we came to a forest. There we dismounted and read the fourth chapter of the Book of Acts, and had a season of prayer. We then again mounted the one horse, and rode on quite a number of miles to the house of a relative of Bro. Jones. There we stopped for the night.

After supper we had a season of worship. I felt led to speak at length,-stood up and did so. At the end of the discourse the head of the family and his wife came forward, and I professed faith in Christ Jesus as their Saviour. That night was one of very great peace and joy to me. I had quiet communion and fellowship with Christ Jesus, my Lord.

In the morning Bro. Jones was not able to travel. That portion of his body-his back-which had been bruised by the whipping was purple because of the bruising and stagnated blood. I left him, only sorrowing that I had not shared some of his suffering, and thus been brought more fully into sympathy with our once suffering Lord and his then suffering poor. Of this experience I was conscious.

Alone I started for my home, some ten or twelve miles distant. Terror had spread its pall over all the country. No glad faces greeted, until I came to my little home. Wife and children were glad to see me,- wife not apparently surprised nor dismayed. Violent persecution was to both of us no new thing; it had been of frequent occurrence during the past twelve years.

I had anticipated something of this, when, fifteen years previously, I had entered into covenant with God to preach in this, my native State, this gospel of love, of justice, of liberty. I had then counted the cost, and did not then, nor in the hands of any mob, have to decide what to do.

In these trials my wife was more cheery than I. This cheered life's pathway. I did not habitually rejoice as it was my privilege and duty to do. (See Matt. 5:12.)

We remained at our home in great quietude for two days. I then took my horse and rode to Richmond, the county seat, and engaged the services of two lawyers to aid Bro. Jones in the prosecution of the leaders of the mob. I chose to make the prosecution in his behalf rather than in my own. He was regarded as a Republican, and I as a "Radical." I also thought that in this way I would secure Mr. Clay's co-operation, and addressed a letter to him, requesting his aid in behalf of Bro. Jones. He declined, saying, "To do so would be only 'robbing Peter to pay Paul,' " and then advised me to leave the county. He kindly offered to take care of my family and property.

I returned home. Speedily large numbers of the mob came to Richmond, and, as I was informed, swore they would give five hundred lashes to the lawyer who would dare to defend Fee or Jones. As a matter of fact, no prosecution was made. The Circuit Judge, a kind man, afterward a Republican, witnessed the bravado of the threatening mob; the Grand Jury took no notice of the occurrence; the civil arm was paralyzed by the slave power.

A crisis came to Berea. For weeks there was a reign of terror. The male members of the church, with others who were friends, held three formal councils, to which I was invited. These men entreated that I leave; saying, "There is an overwhelming feeling against you; your friends cannot protect you; the mob will kill you and destroy your property." I replied, "I came here to do my duty, and when the mob shall come they will find me at my post."

For weeks, not a man came through our little rustic gate, save Otis B. Waters, the teacher, and "Ham" Rawlings, the tried friend oft referred to. He would come "every few days," and on leaving, would say, "Quist (Christ) was a Wadical (Radical)," and drop large tears of affection over our little children as he was bidding them "good-by."

These were dark days,-days in which we could walk only by faith, not by sight,-taught to "endure as seeing Him who is invisible."

I kept up appointments for preaching in the school-house. For a time the congregation was composed of women, save one or two male members. Some men who were friends stood around in the forest, some with guns near by.

After a time fears subsided, a few men came in, some souls were converted, the little school went on until the close of the term. Then Bro. Waters returned to Oberlin, Ohio, to further prosecute his studies in preparation for the Gospel ministry.

It was notoriously true that sudden destruction came upon the leaders of these latter mobs, as had been true in Lewis, Mason and Bracken Counties. Here in Madison County, one of the violent men in the mob was stabbed six times and fell dead; another was shot in his yard; another shot whilst sitting in his house; another stabbed, and after lingering some days died.

So of the Dripping Spring mob:-two of the leading violent men were shot; a third cut to pieces with a bowie-knife. So in the Rockcastle mob the destruction came speedily and numerous. Men of that reckless class faintly saw a providence, and among themselves banded around the saying, "Old Master is against us."

CHAPTER VI.

Coming of J. A. R. Rogers.-Visit of C. M. Clay.-His Expediencies.-The first Commencement. Adoption of a Constitution.-Caste.-Sectarianism.-Decision to Raise Funds.-Visit to the Imprisoned Mother.-Address in Plymouth Church.-Expulsion of Teachers and Friends at Berea.-Excitement in Bracken County.-Wife Returns to Berea.-Our Sojourn in Ohio.-Death and Burial of our Son Tappan.-Visit to Berea.

EARLY in the year 1858 Bro. J. A. R. Rogers, a graduate from Oberlin Institute, literary and theological, came to Berea. He was an earnest Christian worker. He saw something of the future power of the proposed school. He entered at once into this, and by his efficiency and enthusiasm brought it into high repute. Pupils flocked in from Madison and adjacent counties.

The closing exhibition of the school, under the supervision of Bro. Rogers, was at hand. On the day preceding this exhibition, Cassius M. Clay had an appointment to deliver an address to the people of Berea and vicinity. He had not been at Berea since our difference of opinion at Slate Lick, July 4, 1856. Not many persons were present, and in the defense of his conservative position he was without his former enthusiasm. After the address he walked with me into the woodland, then before my door, and as we sat down on a log, he remarked, "Fee, things look better than I thought they would. I am in heart as much a higher law man as you are, and if we were in Massachusetts we could carry it out; but here we cannot." I replied, "The utterance of moral truth should not be confined to geographical limits, especially in a national canvass."

The reader will allow me to here say, that, in my judgment, this notion of expediency in the non-utterance of moral truth, lest it should seem to hinder success, as exhibited in this remark of Mr. Clay's, was the great mistake of his life, and that it took from him that moral power that was necessary for success, and did more at that time to hinder his advancement to the highest position which the people of this nation could give, than any other cause.

Take as another illustration of his expediencies-his going to the war with Mexico. At the time of his enlistment he was editing the True American, published then in Lexington, Ky. His exposition of the evils of slavery was just; his style vigorous; and his courage admired by all lovers of liberty. No star in the horizon of the American people was rising so rapidly. In his manly journal he had denounced the aggression upon Mexico as a scheme for the extension of American slavery; and yet, whilst editing the most effective journal in the nation, and enrapturing crowded audiences by his lectures on the "social and political evils of slavery," he volunteered to go into that war, waged for the wicked intent-"the extension of slavery." He went;

was captured, imprisoned, returned. He expected an ovation. Such as he had hoped for he did not receive.

He said to me, "Fee, I expected by going to Mexico to convince the South that I was not their enemy, but the enemy of slavery; but they gave me no thanks for it." However wise he may have thought his enlistment was, the nation saw that it was "doing evil that good might come."

This apprehension of the people threw him out of line with the moral element that was then moving the nation to the overthrow of slavery-to victory in the line, not of expediencies, but of absolute right.

It is sometimes true that a man must "stand still and see the salvation of God"-commit himself to that only which God can use, the absolute right, and then work and wait until God can vindicate the right. Then the man will have the confidence of righteous men,-the only men God can use as the true builders of His work. Then will he have that conscious unity with God that gives quiet, true courage and endurance; then, too, he will be kept from drifting into other departures from God and right-his "seed," his holy purpose to be one with God and the right, "remaineth in him" to keep him.

The narrative concerning Saul was written for our admonition and instruction. He had at one time a commanding position. God, through his prophet, told Saul, as God's minister and the executive of the nation, to go and "hew down the Amalekites,-

men, women and children; ox and sheep." Saul spared Agag and the best of the sheep and oxen for sacrifice-an attempt to atone for neglect of absolute obedience by a large sacrifice. God said, "To obey is better than sacrifice; and to hearken, than the fat of rams." He took His Spirit and the kingdom from Saul.

Other departures from God and right marked the after career of Saul. So of my friend C. M. Clay; and there will not be safety to any man except as he is anchored fully in God.

We would not have made this personal allusion but for the fact that the struggle with Mr. Clay and his views of expediency were a part, and the severest part, of the history of Berea and its work. Also, we believe that readers, especially the youth, ought to have the benefit of our observations, experiences and suggestions. History should have its lessons.

Mr. Clay at this time was the most conspicuous character in the history of Berea. His known opposition to us was a power more potent and depressing than all the mobs in the State. His position seemed wise to many, whilst that of the mobs was at all times simply brutish and cowardly. Also, at that time, Mr. Clay had a national reputation for courage, patriotism, philanthropy, and a high social position. With all this he was as strong in condemning my position as he had been previously free in commending. He took pains to publish to the world that he had "denounced Mr. Fee's position," (though he had substantially conceded it at the Slate Lick celebration, and had confessed that he was with me "in heart,") and that my position was "insurrectionary, revolutionary and dangerous"; though I had been careful to say, "I make no rebellion, or armed resistance-only, exercise my province as a minister for God to utter moral truth-that human slavery is contrary to natural right, and, as such, statutes enforcing it are without the elements of true law, exist by mere usurpation, and are confessedly contrary to the law of God, and as such ought not by human courts to be enforced."

Mr. Clay did not intend to misrepresent, but only to state his opinion of what would be the tendency of my utterances. This opinion of his was, at that time, a great weight-a weight to be endured, until God, by His providence, should "break every yoke, and let the oppressed go free." This He did, and then everybody said, Amen.

Also; Mr. Clay's objection to the co-education of the "races"-the impartial feature of the school and church at Berea-was well known. He did not believe such a school could be a numerical or a financial success Also he feared evil results to virtue. We had then no sufficient precedent to guide, and no theory to maintain, save that it is always safe to do right-follow Christ; and we knew He would not turn away anyone who came seeking knowledge, even if "carved in ebony." We knew that whilst He is a respecter of character, he is not of persons. As His followers, there was to us but the one course to pursue-open the school to all of virtuous habits.

Also we believed that the best way to inspire woman, colored or white, with virtuous sentiments, and establish in her habits of purity, was not to treat her invidiously-shut her up in pens, schools, by herself, but treat her like other women of respectability and thus inspire her with hope and noble resolve, and lift her above the seductive influences of a vicious life. In other words, practice the Golden Rule-"do unto all as you would they should do unto you."

The wisdom of following this rule has been verified in the history of the school and church at Berea, and we have occasion to know that Mr. Clay greatly rejoices in this fact. Mr. Clay thought that he was pursuing the wisest course, but he was misled, as many are now, by his notions of expediency.

There were other facts of interest connected with the closing exercises of the first term of the school in 1858, indicating a change of public sentiment, and strong sympathy with the school, and kind regard for those conducting it.

In the grove in front of the school-room a large and beautiful bower had been prepared, and hand-bills posted, announcing the order of exercises for the forenoon, and the speakers for the afternoon. The sun on the 24th day of June, unveiled by a single cloud, rose upon us in great beauty and glory. All around was quiet and lovely. Nature was arrayed in her most beautiful dress. At an early hour the people came from this and adjoining counties to witness the exhibition. At the appointed hour the exercises were opened by singing from well-trained voices, and by prayer to Almighty God for his guidance and blessing.

The valedictory, the closing address of the school, was delivered by a young man, bright in intellect, amiable in spirit, and upright in conduct; the son of a man who was first in the formation of the church at Berea, and in every good work. That only and loved son fell on the battlefield at Bellmont, Mo. In his allusion to teachers and fellow-students, he was completely overcome with emotion, and many in the audience were moved to tears.

An excellent dinner had been prepared and spread on long tables in the grove. All were invited to partake. Among those who partook were men who had been engaged in former mobs. Without any ostentation they were kindly treated, and they seemed to appreciate the kindness.

Dr. Chase, a native of New Hampshire, and a relative of S. P. Chase, once Secretary of U. S. Treasury, was there. He was then a practicing physician in this county, and was announced as the first speaker. As he came upon the platform, a portly and venerable-looking man from an adjoining county, and an ex-member of the State legislature, arose in the audience and cried out, "Dr. Chase, I want to speak, and to speak now; for I cannot tarry until your exercises are all through." Dr. Chase gave place. The ex-legislator, then the owner of quite a number of slaves, came on to the platform, and began by saying, "When I came up here with my friend Mason," (another slaveholder and then a citizen of this county,) "I expected to see a little handful in the bresh," (brush,) "but when I saw this large assembly, orderly, and listening with marked attention and interest, and when I saw the marked progress of these pupils, and the manifest sympathy between teachers and pupils, my heart was touched. I thought of the days when I was a teacher of youth in Virginia."

Turning to parents, he said, "Teach your children to make their bread by the sweat of their brow; give them education, and teach them virtue and morality; and the best of all rules is, 'Whatsoever ye would that men should do unto you, do ye even so to them.'" To such utterances, on such an occasion, we were not averse. The rest of his short address was pertinent and good.

He stepped from the platform, and walking to the outskirts of the crowd, he met an old acquaintance, then a patron of the school, and taking him by the hand said, "Jimmy, I believe in my soul the 'niggers' will be free yet; but, d--n it, I mean to hold on to mine as long as I can." He did; but in 1864, Uncle Sam came along and gave them all a blue coat.

After this unexpected episode in the closing exercises of the school, Dr. Chase and others made addresses, and the large and orderly assembly dispersed, evidently deeply impressed in favor of Christian education-slavery or no slavery. The outlook, on that day, was good for Berea.

Hundreds now continue to express their surprise at the interest manifested by the people at the commencement exercises of Berea College. Usually from three to five thousand people attend. Two-thirds of these are white. The large tabernacle, which seats some two thousand people, will not seat more than half the people who come. Good order generally prevails. The delivery on the platform of essays and orations from colored and white students, male and female, is an educational force to the thousands who attend.

In all these efforts there was a continuous purpose to establish in interior Kentucky a college for the education of the youth of the land. Adverse circumstances had all the while been threatening to thwart any such effort. These, however, only served to make more apparent the necessity of such an educational agency, and to make strong the purpose of its original projectors.

Now that possibly the severest effort to intimidate had passed by, and the reaction in favor of liberty and education was manifest, it was deemed wise to make an advance movement. Accordingly, as shown in the minutes of the conventions that devised ways and means to the end, on Sept. 7, 1858, John G. Fee, J. A. R. Rogers, John G. Hanson, John Smith, Wm. Stapp, and John Burnham, Sr., met at the study of John G. Fee, and after prayer and consultation appointed J. A. R. Rogers, John Smith and Wm. Stapp a committee to draft Preamble and Constitution, to be considered at next meeting, which meeting was held Dec. 1,

1858. At this meeting the proposed Constitution was considered, and after some modification adopted. Other meetings were held, a board of trustees was appointed, and officers were elected as follows: John G. Fee, president; J. A. R. Rogers, vice-president; John G. Hanson, secretary; T. E. Renfro, treasurer.

Other meetings of the board followed, additional trustees were added, and on July 14, 1859, the Constitution was reaffirmed and by-laws adopted. It was the firm belief of the projectors of this college that an institution designed for the education of youth should not merely teach the classics and so-called natural sciences, but also moral science-the religion of the Bible, that puts man in harmony with God and His laws in reference to the government of man-that science that teaches that God is the source of all true law, that men are only legislators, that is, law bringers, as the word imports; and that man, universal man, is entitled to the full benefit of these laws.

It was to be expected that a Constitution with by-laws for the government of such an institution, would be in harmony with such sentiments. The first by-law declared, "The object of this college shall be to furnish the facilities for thorough education to all persons of good moral character." The second by-law was more specific, and is as follows: "This college shall be under an influence strictly Christian, and as such, opposed to sectarianism, slave-holding, caste, and every other wrong institution or practice." Opposition to caste meant the co-education of the (so-called) "races." This has been the continued practice of the college.

There were some of the friends of liberty who could assent to the general principles of justice and love, who thought it not expedient to make a literal, specific application of them; that whilst the rule, "do unto men as you would that they should do unto you," was a good rule in general, it was not expedient to practice upon it in the co-education of the races.

Among these was our friend, C. M. Clay. He declined to act as a trustee. Soon two, and then after a time a third one of those who first agreed to be trustees, dropped out. Thus the caste issue sifted the very board of trustees themselves.

There were many others who were opposed to slavery and desired the entire liberty of the negro, yet were unprepared to give to him that position which merit required, and which is a great incentive to noble and virtuous conduct. Such Christ-like treatment would tend to the harmony of society, the solidification of the social forces of the nation, and present a proper exhibition of the Gospel of Christ, who is Himself no respecter of persons. (He is of character-not of persons.) The incorporation of the principle of impartial conduct to all, in institutions for the public good, was to the founders of Berea College the only course at once Christian, patriotic, and philanthropic. This now incorporated feature of the college made the school, and community in which it was nestled, still more odious to an unregenerate public sentiment; and as we shall hereafter notice, subjected us to still greater outrages.

Another hindrance to reform and progress was sectarianism. The founders of the college saw that in every community where they, raised their voices against slavery, caste, secretism, rum-selling, any popular vice, immediately members of the sects would be found shrinking from the proclamation of truth and the utterance of their own convictions, lest by so doing they should peril the safety of their sects, or denominations. With the semblance of piety they would say, "Peace is best," and thus smother truth. The founders also saw that everywhere the shelves of libraries and book-stores were bending beneath the volumes written on theological dogmas, whilst "truth [practical truth] was fallen in the streets, and equity could not enter." Ministers were spending their energies in zealous debates and fervid, eloquent pleadings over the shibboleths of party, whilst the slave was groaning in his bondage, and the masters were deluded with false hopes and a perverted Bible.

The founders of Berea College not only felt that the fountains of all good, of true religion, should be opened, but that the great barrier, sectarianism, should be removed. They also saw that no influence is so potent for the removal of error and the establishment of truth, as that of chartered institutions, having the prestige of men of learning and piety. They resolved "that Berea College should be under an influence strictly Christian, and, as such, opposed to sectarianism, slave-holding, caste, and every other wrong institution and practice." In declaring that the institution should be opposed to sectarianism, the trustees, as explained in the minutes of the meeting that adopted the Constitution and by-laws, were careful and explicit; saying, "In the election of president, professors, or teachers, no sectarian test shall be applied, but it shall be required that the candidate be competent to fill the office, and have a Christian experience with a righteous practice."

The trustees further added, "To be anti-sectarian is to oppose everything that causes schism in the body of Christ, or among those who are Christians,- those who have a Christian experience with a righteous practice"; so that it is requisite that a president, professor, or teacher of Berea College be not merely negative on this issue,-simply not sectarian, but positive,-that he shall oppose sectarianism as he would slave-holding, caste, rum-selling, or any other "wrong practice."

To help in the removal of the sin of schism is one of the missions of Berea College, and no person as "president, professor or teacher," is faithful to the spirit or letter of the Constitution of the college who adopts or defends sectarianism,-yea, does not oppose and seek to correct the "evil practice." The interests of society and the kingdom of Christ require this.

The Constitution and by-laws of Berea College having been adopted, the trustees decided to raise funds and erect buildings for school purposes as speedily as possible. With the consent of the trustees, the prudential committee, composed of J. G. Fee, J. A. R. Rogers, J. G. Hanson, and Thomas Renfro, decided that, making themselves personally responsible, they would contract for 117 acres of land, including the present site of Berea College, and that on which part of the village of Berea now stands. Soon after the information of this purchase I went to Worcester, Mass., to attend the annual meeting of the American Missionary Association. The Association was at that time undenominational, and not doing avowedly the work of any one denomination, as it now is doing.

I decided that on my way to Worcester, Mass., I would take my family to visit Julett Miles, the imprisoned mother, yet in the State's prison at Frankfort, Ky., as narrated in chapter third.

We arrived at Frankfort on Saturday afternoon. We went to the prison and saw the keeper, Mr. South. We inquired for "Julett," the colored woman sent there from Bracken County for attempting to get her children into freedom. "Yes," said he, "she is at my house. I took her out of prison to help my daughter. I thought she looked like a Christian woman." The reader will note the fact that men and women were deemed valuable in proportion as they had Christ in them,-in proportion as they were temples of the Holy Spirit,-they were the more trustworthy. The keeper of the prison having assured us that we should see the woman at the prison the next morning, we then repaired to our hotel.

That night, leaving my wife with the three smaller children at the hotel, I took Laura, my daughter, then fourteen years old, and went to the colored Baptist church, and listened to a very effective sermon delivered by a portly, fine-looking colored man, whose name was Monroe. I was present in the early part of the services. I heard the earnest prayers, the familiar songs, the low, plaintive symphonies of the women,-of mothers whose bosoms had been the seats of sorrows. I had heard these low wailings before; but a series of experiences, and my situation at that time, all conspired to bring me more fully into sympathy with the sorrowing. I sat and quietly wept-wept with continuous weeping. I was in deep sympathy with burdened spirits. At the close of the service I went forward and shook hands with the preacher, and told him I had been greatly benefited by the service. Laura and I returned to the hotel. The next morning, about 10 o'clock, we all, as a family, went to the prison. "Julett" was there. She was overjoyed at seeing my children. She had always manifested much affection for them. We were privileged to sit down and have a very free and extended conversation with her about her nine children, their unknown destiny, And her own future.

We then inquired of the keeper for Calvin Fairbanks, a white man, who was then in the prison under sentence for aiding away slaves. We were told that he was in his cell,-"not well." My wife heard the whisper from some one of the employes that he had been whipped and kept in his cell for not completing his task of work the day before. Fairbanks, who usually led the worship in the chapel, not being present, I was requested to conduct the worship. I did so, and preached to the assembled convicts. I had this observation whilst there: that Fairbanks was the leader of worship, and Julett Miles the house maid. The Negro stealers were, by the keeper himself, adjudged as having the highest measure of piety, and therefore given the posts of trust.

The next morning we were privileged to see Fairbanks for a short time. Calvin Fairbanks was a native of the State of New York. He had been sentenced to twenty years imprisonment for aiding slaves to escape. He remained in prison twelve years. During the war, in the absence of the Governor, he was pardoned by the Lieutenant-Governor. He is now living in his native State, honored and loved.

After seeing Fairbanks we had another interview with "Julett." I had procured for her a pair of spectacles and a New Testament, with large type. Giving these to her, we bade her farewell for all time.

Not long after this she died,-disease said to have been of the heart. Thousands of slave-mothers have died with broken hearts, whilst political parties catered to the slave-master, and professing Christians heeded not the wailings of the bereaved.

Is poor, depraved humanity any better now? Are not political parties as servile before the Rum Power, as they were fifty years ago before the Slave Power? Are not the many professing Christians as indifferent to the weepings of the Rachels, who refuse to be comforted because their children and husbands are not?

My wife and three of our children returned to our home in Madison County. I took Laura, our eldest child, and went on to Worcester, Mass., to attend an annual Meeting of the American Missionary Association.

Immediately after the meeting of the Association, I commenced the work of soliciting funds with which to procure lands and erect buildings for Berea College. A few subscriptions were secured at Worcester.

At the suggestion of Lewis Tappan, a request came to me from Henry Ward Beecher, pastor of the Plymouth Church, Brooklyn, N. Y., to come to that church and present the claims of Berea College. This was at the time of the John Brown raid in Western Virginia. The country was in a state of intense excitement.

In my address before the church I said, "We want more John Browns; not in manner of action, but in spirit of consecration; not to go with carnal weapons, but with spiritual; men who, with Bibles in their hands, and tears in their eyes, will beseech men to be reconciled to God. Give us such men," I said, "and we may yet save the South." My words were carefully reported and published in the N. Y. Tribune. The Louisville Courier, then conducted by Geo. D. Prentiss, garbled my words and misrepresented my real attitude by saying, "John G. Fee is in Beecher's church, calling for more John Browns."

These words were copied by the Lexington Observer, published in Lexington, Ky., and by the Mountain Democrat, published in Richmond, Ky. To this first misrepresentation was added a straight-out falsehood-that "at Cogar's landing was found a box of Sharp's rifles directed to John G. Fee." These falsehoods, added to the consciousness that men were sleeping over a magazine, the outraged feelings of thousands, were enough to alarm the slave power. Speedily were gathered into Richmond, the county seat of this county, seven hundred and fifty men-so reported at the time. These pledged themselves to the removal of John G. Fee, J. A. R. Rogers, and their co-laborers, "peaceably if they could, forcibly if they must." A committee of sixty-five, composed of the "wealthiest" and "most respectable" citizens of the county, was commissioned to visit Berea and deliver the demand of those who had decided to take into their control the liberty of white men, as well as that of black men.

I had not yet returned from my trip eastward. The committee, on the 23rd day of Dec., 1859, proceeded to the house of Bro. Rogers, then principal of the school. The leader of the clan delivered to Bro. Rogers a document, demanding in the name of the committee, that he should leave the State within ten days. He attempted to reason with the committee, setting forth his claims as a law-abiding citizen, to the undisturbed exercise of his rights. The committee turned abruptly away, and delivered a like demand to ten other families, most of whom were native Kentuckians. These thus warned to leave the State, and others interested in the work of building up the school and church, met together for prayer and deliberation.

These friends decided at once to make their appeal to the Governor of the State, for protection. This they did, in the form of a short address, borne by two of their number to the Governor, setting forth their obedience to law, and their devotion to the highest interests of society, and as such asked for protection. The Governor replied that the public mind was deeply moved by the events in Virginia, and that he could not engage to protect them from their fellow citizens, who had resolved that they must go. Many of these thus threatened saw that they must yield before an overwhelming force.

After committing themselves to God in humble prayer, most of these thus warned retired from the State, believing that "God would make the wrath of man to praise Him."

At this time I was on my way home from New York. Friends at Berea importuned my wife to go and meet me, if possible, and tell me not to attempt to come home now, for men were waylaying me at three different places. Along with my daughter Laura I met my wife at Cincinnati, Ohio. The next day we met the exiles from Berea. It was deemed wise now to hold meetings in Cincinnati. From this place we went to an appointment, previously made for me, in Bethesda church-house, in Bracken County, Ky. Here, whilst in the stand preaching, some of my exiled children, not previously seen for months, came into the church-house. With these came other exiles. Among them was John G. Hanson and family.

The Monday following this meeting was county court day in Bracken County. Already Bro. Jas. S. Davis had been driven from the church in Lewis County. J. M. Mallett, a teacher in the school at Bethesda, had been mobbed and driven out of Germantown, Bracken County. In sympathy with the slave power, public feeling was at white heat. It was estimated that 800 people gathered on that county court day at Brooksville, the county seat of Bracken County. A special meeting was called. Inflammatory speeches were made, referring to the John Brown raid in Virginia, the expulsion of Abolitionists from Berea, in Madison County, and from the "Abolition" church in Lewis County, and the expulsion of the "Abolitionr" teacher in Bracken County; and now it was claimed that the security of property and peace of society demanded that John G. Fee, John G. Hanson, and others associated with them, be not allowed to tarry, even for a short time, in Bracken County, their native county. Such a resolve against men unconvicted of any crime, present or past, and now in their native county, in the midst of relatives and life-long acquaintances, was as dastardly as it was vile. But the slave power was in its very nature one of oppression and outrage; and the great mass of the non-slave-owners had become servile; and, though not slave-owners, had consented to be slaveholders, and joined with or consented to the demand of the slave-owners. A committee of sixty-two men, of "high standing," was appointed to warn John G. Fee, John G. Hanson and others associated, to leave the county, "peaceably if they would, forcibly if they must." On the day appointed, the committee of sixty-two rode up to the yard fence in front of the dwelling-house of Vincent Hamilton, my father-in-law, where with my wife and children I was then stopping. These men then sent in a request that I come out. I did so, and listened to their resolutions. The committee then demanded from me a reply. I said, as my custom was on such occasions, "I make no pledges to surrender God-given and constitutional rights to any man or set of men. If I shall be convicted of crime, before an impartial jury, then I will submit to adequate punishment." I then proceeded with further defense of my claim to citizenship and free speech, when the captain of the band ordered, "Forward, march."

One of these men I took by the arm. He had been a member of the State Legislature. In his house my wife, in girlhood days, had boarded whilst attending school. With his sons I had studied in the school-room and played on the playground. This man was then an elder in the Presbyterian "church" at Sharon church-house, where my wife and I, years previously, had made profession of faith in Christ, and from the hands of this man we had received the emblems of the broken body and shed blood of our Lord. I referred to these things, and said to him, "Is this the treatment that we, convicted of no crime, should expect from one who has known us from childhood, with whom we have lived as neighbors, and who is now an office-bearer in a professedly Christian church?" He replied, "It is not worth while for us to talk," and rode off in pursuit of the committee-men. These committee-men served a like notice upon J. G. Hanson and others.

At first I thought I would not go from Bracken County, though it was not then my home. I had so expressed myself. Two members of the church there, John D. Gregg and John Humlong, men whose courage, fidelity and piety perhaps no man questioned, said, "Our first impulse was to take our rifles and stand with you; but other friends warned to leave have decided to go, and we find that we will be utterly overwhelmed by the opposing power, and if you stay we shall all be driven away." My father-in-law made the same remark. This put a new phase on the issue. I might peril my own home, and had done so. I might no peril the home of another, especially when he had expressed his fear. A day of fasting and prayer was appointed, and a meeting of brethren and sisters in Christ was held at the church-house. The conclusion was, "There is now such a reign of terror all over the State that you cannot get a hearing anywhere in the State." The same was the response from friends in Madison County. Thus persecuted, the admonition seemed pertinent, "When they persecute you in this city, flee ye into another." I said, "It is possible I cannot reach my own home, and could not get the friends together, even if there; but 'tis a time not to be silent." Therefore, John G. Hanson, myself and others, retired with our families for a time to the North and took up our abode in the suburbs of Cincinnati, Ohio.

Notwithstanding the intense excitement in the country, my wife believed she could get back to our home and get out our household goods. Accordingly, taking a carriage and our eldest son, then ten years old, she started, and on the third day, after overcoming severe difficulties, reached her home. She boxed up our goods, shipped them to Cincinnati, and returned to her father's house. From thence, with her children, she came to me, into a house I had secured near to Cincinnati, Ohio.

Soon after this my youngest son, Tappan, then four years old, from exposure in the exodus in mid-winter, took a cold, which culminated in diphtheria and death. This was an hour of great sadness. With the impression that I would yet return to my fields of labor in Kentucky, and as Joseph requested that his bones be taken back to Canaan, so with this Scripture in my mind, I decided to carry back the body of my dear boy, "bone of my bone, and flesh of my flesh," and thus strengthen my purpose to return, and my claim upon this, my native soil and field of labor, chosen in sacred covenant years previously. In great sorrow I brought the dear form and buried it in the little graveyard adjoining Bethesda church-house-a place ever dear to me.

After the interment of the dear body we returned to Ohio. A few weeks later my wife and I returned to Bracken County, Ky., bringing with us head and foot stones with which to mark the resting-place of our dear boy.

Soon after leaving the boat that landed us at the town of Augusta, I was surrounded by a mob, a gathering of citizens, many of whom considered themselves respectable people; and for a time I was not allowed to proceed farther. The only cause of this detention was mere hostility to me as a known Abolitionist. I had been born and reared in that county, and had preached to the people at Bethesda most of the ten preceding years. No man could prefer a charge of crime, and the object of my visit was humane and Christian. Detention under such circumstances was an outrage too gross; and after a time I

was allowed to go on my way. I visited the grave of my child, preached on Lord's day, and, after a day or two, returned to my family, then in Ohio.

The unfinished work on my hands was the collection of money with which to pay for the land previously bought, as a site for Berea College. This money I succeeded in raising, and paid for the land on which most of the buildings of Berea College now stand.

By this time the rebellion became imminent. The enmity on the part of many so-called Union men was more intense against Abolitionists than against rebels themselves. By many undiscerning men, the Abolitionists were charged with bringing on the war-precipitating the great calamity. This charge was as senseless as that of those who, with Ingersoll, charge Christianity with the persecutions waged by paganism and the papacy. Nevertheless, passion raged. The most that could be done was still to call upon the nation to obey God and "let the oppressed go free";-remove slavery, the festering cause. This, neither political party then intended to do. The cry on both sides was, "a white man's war"-"let the nigger stay where he is."

Even Abraham Lincoln then said, "Let us save the Union, slavery or no slavery."

The Bull Run defeat came, and one reverse after another. The "before breakfast spell" of Wm. H. Seward lasted months and years. Slowly the people began to think that they must obey God, must "break every yoke and let the oppressed go free";-that it was folly to attempt to conquer a people in their own territory and in their own fastnesses, without a vastly superior force. John C. Fremont had the sagacity to see this and act upon it. He made a proclamation of freedom to slaves in his department. The President of the nation, as commander-in-chief, revoked the proclamation as premature. The step taken by Fremont was in the right direction; and one from which the heart and judgment of the discerning part of the nation did not go back. Some of us thought we saw in this "the beginning of the end"-that blood and treasure was not henceforth to be spent in vain.

Physical disability at this time forbade my entering the army and bearing arms. I also had a conviction that there must be a change of public sentiment before there would be a vigorous change of tactics; and that therefore my work was moral rather than physical; and that I must give myself to this in the most effective way-must do what I could to change public sentiment in free and slave States.

After some months I said to my wife, "Let us go out into Kentucky on a tour of inspection and see for ourselves actual condition of society there." We came to Berea. We found John Morgan raiding the country, and society in a turmoil: still we found a few friends, natives of the State, who were here, and not wholly discouraged. We decided to go back, gather up our children, and come out to Berea and resume our previously-chosen, and, in purpose, never relinquished work.

CHAPTER VII.

Effort to Get Back.-Battle at Richmond, Ky.-Again Mobbed at Augusta, Ky.-Mobbed at Washington, Ky.-Return of my Wife to Berea. Her Stay There.-Return to the Border.-Stay at Parker's Academy.-Return to Berea.-Resumption of the Work.-Moved to go to Camp Nelson.-My Work There.

We came up to Bracken County, and my wife, taking her horse and carriage, took the two eldest children and started across the country for Berea. I took the younger son and started around by Cincinnati, that I might there arrange for the publication of another anti-slavery tract, and also ship our household goods back to Berea. I found that our goods could not then be shipped. The government had the entire use of the railroad in shipping munitions of war. My son and I got as far as Richmond, Ky. There I engaged a single horse on condition that I would not take the horse into rebel lines. We mounted the horse,-Howard behind me, and came seven miles toward our home.

We there met the Union forces retreating before the advance of Kirby Smith's invading army. Some Union troops were gathered at and near to Richmond. These resisted the approach of the rebel army, but were over-powered and fell back to Richmond, thence to Lexington, and afterwards dispersed in various directions. I fell back with the Union forces to Lexington, and from thence to

Bracken County. There I left my son Howard, then eleven years old, with his grandfather. I went on to Augusta, a town on the Ohio river, intending, if possible, to get around to my wife and the other children, then at Berea.

Whilst waiting on the wharf for the down packet I was there seized by a mob and brought up into the town and taken into the office of Dr. Josh Bradford, a man who professed to be a Union man, and was then helping to raise a regiment of men. These professedly Union men hated Abolitionists more than they did the rebels. They demanded that I pledge to leave the State and never come back again. I said, "I make no pledges to men." A great crowd was outside. Bradford, a relative on my father's side, went out, and soon returned, and calling me by name, said, "We are going to put you across the river, and if you come back again I will hang you if it be the last act of my life." I said, "Do your duty, and I will try to do mine." Eight of the company took me to a flat boat, which they had in readiness. They suffered no others to get into the boat. As the crowd turned away I heard the leader say, "We will whip him like hell." They started off for other boats,-skiffs. The eight men put me across the river. As the boat struck the shore on the Ohio side I stepped on to the shore, and seeing the rabble as pursuers lower down the river, I walked quickly up the bank, and seeing a cornfield before me leaped the fence and was soon out of sight of pursuers. I could hear the men who were seeking for me passing up and down the banks. I passed across the field and ascended the hill rising from the banks on the Ohio side. I sat down. It was now the month of August.

The moon was full, and shone brightly on "Olimba's silver wave." Over on the opposite side was the town of Augusta. There stood the old college building, where for years I had pursued the early part of my college course. There, too, was the little brick building where my wife, boarding with her aunt, had spent part of her early school days. I said, Why am I thus an exile, and hunted like a wild beast? I have injured no man. I have violated no law. My only offense is that I have plead for the slave, and ask that men obey the command of their Lord, "Do unto men as ye would that they do unto you." I thought of my wife and children far in the interior of the State, in the midst of rebel forces, and there without bread to eat or a bed on which to sleep, only as others might share with them.

I did not dare compare myself with our Lord; but I thought of him in Nazareth, where those who were relatives, and knew him from childhood, sought to kill him,-dash him headlong over a deadly precipice.

I sat there thinking of the slave-father, sundered far from his wife and children, with no hope of ever seeing them again. I then said, A loving Father will overrule all this for good. I shall be the better prepared for my work, and by these and like events moral forces will be prepared by which good will break this system of iniquity to pieces as a potter's vessel is broken.

At early dawn I left the spot of commanding view, and the place of mingled sorrow and joy, and went down to the house of a friend, and the mother of one who had been with me as college mate. With this mother and family I took breakfast. By first down boat I went down to Covington, Ky., and out into Lew. Wallace's camp. He had here the command of Union forces by which to prevent the advance of Kirby Smith's army on to Cincinnati. After a few days I went to Oberlin, Ohio, that I might there attend a meeting of the American Missionary Association.

From Oberlin I came back to Bracken County, Ky., and to the house of my father-in-law. Taking my son, Howard, I came up to Washington, Mason County, hoping there to take the stage coach. We went to the house of a Presbyterian minister who had often been at my father's house, and with whom I had often broken bread around the table of our Lord. This man was not at home when we first went to his house, and stage time having not yet come, we tarried.

When the minister arrived I saw I was not a welcome guest. He soon said, "I am sorry you are here"; and then turning said, "Do you see those men gathering?" I had not noticed them. He added, "They do not intend to let you pass." Soon the men were in his yard and had surrounded me. The preacher said, "Some of these men are members of my church. They will not hurt you." Resistance was useless,-escape impossible. We were surrounded and borne along down into the town. The crowd continued to increase, and it became manifest they could not afford to stay there all night. I had committed no breach of the peace; there could be no legal action against me, and the question arose, "What shall we do with him?" The decision was, "Take him back to Augusta." At that place I had been previously in the hands of two different mobs; and I had no desire to be hauled twelve or fifteen miles at that hour of night, in order to revisit the town of Augusta.

The captain of the crowd ordered his slave man to go out to his farm and bring horse and spring wagon. Whether by design or otherwise, the slave was a long time gone. In the meantime young B., the captain of the crowd, was boasting his courage at the bar of the hotel near by. At length the team came, and further preparations were being made.

All this while my then little son was moving to and fro in the crowd, hearing each word and watching each action. This quiet vigilance, together with the manifest injustice to me, touched the sympathy and aroused the indignation of a noble man who stood as a spectator. He occupied a high social position, and yet lives, and loves to inquire about that "little boy." He determined to protect the boy and save me from the proposed outrage. He communicated his purpose to three others who felt as he did, and they agreed to aid him. When the team was ready, he and his men offered their service to the captain, and stepped into the wagon. In a few moments we were off and the team moving rapidly on.

When the team came to the road leading off to Augusta, friend H. took hold of the lines and said, "No! let's take him to Maysville and deliver him up to Judge C."

This, to the then drunken owner of the team, seemed like "business." He yielded. Our friend kept the reins, and soon we were in Maysville, and in the room of Judge C. The Judge, having over me no jurisdiction, after a friendly shake hands with me took the young drunken man aside and told him what might be the serious consequences of his action. I and my son tendered our friend H. our thanks for his kind interposition, and we walked down the street, and crossed over the river to a quiet hotel in the town opposite, slept well, arose in the morning, took breakfast, and then returned to Maysville, on the Kentucky side, and conferred with friends. I was assured that I could not travel in Kentucky at that juncture, and that my family was safer without me than with me, and that what Union men were left about Berea, were either seized and paroled, or carried off into rebel States. If any escaped these conscriptions, they were so only as they were for the time hid in the caves and the mountains. It seemed to be the part of wisdom that I tarry until the "cloud should rise."

Ten weeks had elapsed since I had seen my wife and the two eldest children. These were weeks of commotion, anxiety and peril. As previously stated, when I started around by Cincinnati, my wife, with her two children, had started in her private carriage across the country for our inland home. The country at that time was full of soldiers, Union and Rebel. The first day she came as far as five miles south of Blue Licks, a noted "watering-place." The next day, after long delays, because of soldiery and government teams, she came to a country store and "tavern"-eighteen miles from her home. The next morning, after securing a small supply of groceries for a destitute home in a destitute region, she started for home. On coming through Richmond, our county seat, the people, men and women, expressed surprise at seeing a woman driving along the highway. She had not proceeded more than three miles when she was halted by Union pickets, who at first suspected she might be a rebel spy, conveying news to Kirby Smith's men, who were already near to her home. Her frank manner, her commendation of "eternal vigilance as the price of liberty," her story of who she was and where she was going, together with the Union flag painted on her carriage, and manifestly, not recently, painted for effect, but of previous design- all these considerations constrained the officer to say, "Let her go; she is all right." She came to her humble home, constructed a bedstead, filled a tick with straw, borrowed a blanket to sleep under, lay down with her two children and slept. The next day whilst out hunting up some simple cooking utensils which two years previously she had distributed among neighbors, rebel soldiers came into her house, took her borrowed blanket, her coarse and fine comb, her better shoes and Burritt's hat, and the carriage harness. The horse and carriage were hid in the woods. My daughter Laura had a very nice Union flag which her mother had made, and with this a set of silver spoons her grandfather had given to her; these she had hid up in the eaves-trough. These the rebels did not find; so the present loss of the little family was not great, and they could say with Col. Slack's slave, "Blessed be nothing; I has nothing to lose, and nothing to be sorry for."

Thousands of Kirby Smith's men were then encamped near by. With some other women my wife went to the encampment to see the complexion of the rebel soldiery. Whilst sitting with other women a rebel officer rode up, and addressing himself politely, inquired of my wife for her home, and then for the "politics" of the region. My wife said, "My home is near by; and, as for politics, we are for the Union, and believe slavery is wrong, and that the rebels are fighting for a lost cause."

The officer inquired, "Madam, ain't you from the North?" She replied, "No, this is my home and my native State." Again he inquired in a tone derisive, "Madam, are you an Abolitionist?" She replied, "I am." "Well," said he, "I have seen some men who were Abolitionists, but I never before this saw a woman who was." My wife then asked, "Why are you here with the uniform of our men on you?" He had a Union belt on him with U. S. inverted. He replied, "Madam, don't you see that is S.U.-Southern Union?" and rode off. Not long after this she heard the Cannon's roar at Perrysville. Soon this was followed by the retreating rebel army with trains of wagons laden with plunder, and herds of lowing cattle famishing for the want of water.

Three rebel officers came up to her house and asked for food. My wife had some potatoes, meal, coarse flour and milk. She gave to them bread and milk, with baked potatoes. They received this kindly, and were very respectful. Soon after they were gone my wife learned that some rebel soldiers were in her potato patch, grabbling her potatoes.

A friend who had occupied the house for a time, left for her a small plat of ground planted with potatoes. Taking her son Burritt with her, she went for her potatoes. Something to live on then was an item of concern. She came to the fence and said, "Men, I have fed your officers, and now you are taking the last potato I have; this is no credit to you." One young fellow looked up pertly and. said, "Madam, credit has gone up long ago." They filled their haversacks and went on.

Scenes of privation, anxiety and toil went on from day to day. At the end of ten weeks my wife's mother came, informing her where I was, and helped her and the children back to the border of the State.

In Kentucky society was in turmoil. There was no opportunity for consecutive work. We passed over into Clermont County, Ohio, put our children into Parker's Academy, and tarried there some months ourselves, and found true friends whom we shall ever hold dear.

After a few months the government began in some of the Gulf States the work of enlisting colored men. I then began to have hope of a speedy and successful termination of the war. I had from the beginning of the war continuously said, "I do not believe we will succeed until we begin enlisting men as men,-not merely white men." With this dawning light I said to my wife, "We will try it again; gather our children and go to Berea." To this place we came in 1864.

The friends previously exiled had not yet returned. With a desire to keep alive the original purpose, and to resuscitate, to some extent, the school previously broken up, I gathered together, as far as possible, the children of the few sympathizing families, took charge of a class myself, and committed the other classes to my wife and eldest daughter.

Soon after this arrangement, whilst sitting in my study, thinking of the political and social condition around me, these words came to me with wonderful force, "Prepare thy work without, and make it fit for thyself in the field; and afterwards build thine house." Prov. 24:27. I did not remember to have seen the text before; but of course I had, in general reading, though at that moment I was not reading my Bible. The text came to me in such manner and with such force, that I could not but regard it as from the Spirit of God; and therefore a call to the work indicated.

The thing indicated to me was this: Until the work on the battlefield shall be first settled, there will be no permanency, or marked progress in your work here, either in school or church;-go do your part.

That part, as I then believed, was moral, religious; rather than physical,-the actual bearing of arms. I had hitherto no confidence that the government would succeed, until it began to "break every yoke and let the oppressed go free"; until it began to enlist men as men,-and not merely as white men. I also knew that just at that time colored men were being enlisted in Kentucky. I believed I knew more about the movements of the government and the feelings of the people North, than these colored men did, and that there were reasons why I could instruct, comfort and encourage them,-reasons why they would hear me, and also reasons why loyal white men would hear me.

Without counsel from, or commission from any board, I immediately prepared to go; took my eldest son, my dear Burritt, then living, and on the next Saturday started for Camp Nelson, thirty-five miles distant.

I found there two regiments of colored men, forming,-not complete. The next day, Lord's day, I mingled freely with these colored soldiers and their officers; and at night preached to a large assemblage of them. This was to me, and to many of these men, a melting occasion. We saw then, in its first unfolding, what we had long and anxiously prayed for,-"the beginning of the end"-the freedom of men, white and colored; freedom in such manner as would give prestige to the latter, and sympathy from the former.

On Monday morning I went to the office of the Quartermaster, then in Camp Nelson, Ky., to secure, if possible, a place for religious service and regular preaching. I found the Quartermaster at his post,-a live man. I told him who I was, and what I wanted. He immediately replied, "I know you,-all about you, and have for years. My home is Holden, Mass. I will give you every facility I can. But," said he, "we want teaching for these colored men as well as preaching. They, especially the non-commissioned officers, need to be taught to write,-sign their names to their reports." I said, "Furnish me a house and desks, and I will secure teachers,-do the work." He agreed to do so. I then went to the commandant of the camp, Gen. S. S. Fry, whose home was then in Danville, Ky. He was and is a Christian gentleman. He gave to the proposed work his hearty endorsement; and within eight days Capt. T. E. Hall, who had three saw-mills and hands "ad libitum" at his command, had enclosed a school-room thirty feet wide and a hundred feet long, furnished with writing tables. Teachers were secured, and the colored soldiers instructed.

At my request Edward Harwood, of Cincinnati, forwarded a large bell,-the bell that now hangs in the belfry of Howard Hall, Berea. This was speedily mounted on a derrick, and at stated hours called soldiers to class, and, at other hours, the people to worship.

I secured instructors for these men. They were intensely eager to learn how to make reports and write their names. Gen. Fry was interested in this help to his soldiery, and occasionally by his personal presence and words of exhortation encouraged the men to efforts of perseverance. There was now no fear that these men would write passports for freedom. They were in the enjoyment of the long-prayed-for boon.

This was a time of thrilling interest to me. There was now not only the fair prospect that the nation would be delivered from the perils of a wicked rebellion, but with this, the freedom of the then five million of slaves. These were now, by the demand of loyal men, and the proclamation of the nation's chief executive, to go forth as free men and free women;-a consummation for which I, in common with others, had long prayed and labored.

The event came in a way we had not prayed for; it came in blood, yet in a way of individual and national peril that overcame former antipathies and race distinction, and engendered mutual sympathies that nothing short of the superabounding grace of God,-another sheet from Heaven to bigoted Peters,-could have overcome.

There were additional thrills of interest to me. I had long been shunned, through fear of others, by those who had a secret sympathy with me, and had long been hated and persecuted by others. Now, to meet the benignant smiles and grateful benedictions of colored men, and the friendly, hearty grasp of hand by loyal white men was a revelation as grateful as new,-to be felt but not described. It was also a providence by which I became personally acquainted with officials and privates, colored and white, and my face and character known to thousands, yet in the State, and a providence by which I can yet do good to them and their children. Nor should any one be surprised if, from associations of the past, I should be greatly attached to that beautiful spot, Camp Nelson; the cradle of liberty to central Kentucky. There the thousands, men, women and children, received their passports from government officials, into that freedom which naturally is the heritage of all men. May that place, as well as Berea, be a fountain of good to the State, and ever free from Rum, Caste, Sect and Secretism. I wish some one, by his or her means, would lift the school and church there into yet higher efficiency.

There was another phase of the work at Camp Nelson, then of interest to me, and connected by principle and effect with the work at Berea. The enlistment of colored men at Camp Nelson was soon followed by the coming of their wives and children. These were at first driven out of the camp at the point of the bayonet. Thus sent back, they were exposed to the cruelty of their former masters. I saw indignation rising in the hearts and showing itself in the actions of the colored soldiers. I went to the officials and said to them, "This driving back of wives and children will breed mutiny in your camp unless you desist." The reply was, "What will you do?-will you leave the women and children with the soldiers? That will never do." I said, "No; I would draw a picket line and put the women in the west end of the camp, which is abundantly large and encircled by Kentucky river and cliffs four hundred feet high. Such a natural fortification, high, beautiful, and well-watered, was not anywhere else found in the State." "But," said the Quartermaster, "I can do nothing in the way of shelter without an order from the Secretary of War." I replied, "I know Secretary Chase personally. I will prepare a paper to be sent to his care." "Do so," said the Quartermaster, "and I will sign it." The paper was forwarded. Quickly an order came from Stanton, the Secretary of War, for the construction of buildings; and in a short time the Quartermaster had ninety-two cottages erected as homes for families, two larger buildings as hospitals for sick women and children, and other buildings as school-rooms and offices, boarding hall, and dormitory for teachers, steward and family.

Spending, as I did, a Sabbath in a neighboring city, I saw in the congregation (colored) a young woman of light complexion, whose manner, as she came to the altar to partake of the Lord's Supper, favorably impressed me. I inquired of the pastor who she was. He told me she was a member of that church, with fair education and good parentage. Immediately it occurred to me that she was the woman with whom to test the caste question among the teachers at Camp Nelson, and set the precedent of giving positions to colored persons as fast as prepared for such. Monday morning I called on her parents and told to them my wish and plan. I suggested to them and the daughter what might be the opposition; but such, I said, would be un-Christ-like, and the sooner met the better, and that perhaps the daughter was "raised up for a time like this." They consented to the arrangement, and on Wednesday the young lady was at the office of the school-building. Immediately I assigned to her a room in the dormitory, and put her in charge of a class of pupils. At the dinner hour I gave to her in the common dining-hall a chair and place at the table at which I presided. The presence of this young lady at one of the several tables in the common dining-hall, produced a sensation. A chaplain to one of the regiments, whose home was down in Maine, together with some army officials also boarding at the hall, protested against this young woman's eating in the common boarding-hall. All the lady teachers (white) sent there by the American Missionary Association and the Freedman's Aid Society, refused, with two exceptions, to come to the first tables whilst the young woman was eating. She was, in person, tidy, modest, comely. It is just to say that the secretaries of the American Missionary Association would not have endorsed the action of those teachers, who thus refused to eat at the common table with such a teacher as the one referred to.

A major, whose home was in Illinois, and the steward, whose home was in the same State, came to me and suggested that I remove the young woman. I saw the moment for decision had come, and in a quiet manner said, "I will suffer my right arm torn from my body before I will remove the young woman." And that they might see that I was not arbitrary in my decision, I said, "The young woman is fitted for her position; she is modest and discreet; she is a Christian, and as such, Christ's representative. What I do to her I do to him." Both of these men were professing Christians, and one of them a local preacher, at home.

The steward said his wife would not give the young woman a plate. I replied, "Then she shall have mine, and I will have another"; for the control had been given to me, and I meant to keep it, and use it.

That one, who was then a young woman, is now the wife of one of the trustees of Berea College. Events, like summer clouds, often cast their shadows before them.

During the latter part of the war, for some fifteen months, I gave most of my time and labor to the work in Camp Nelson, Ky. Whilst there I organized a school and gathered together believers into a church, delivered from rum, secretism and sect. The church and school remain free from rum, sect and secretism up to the present time. I saw then, as now, the importance of such a church and school in that central part of the State; in the midst of an immense colored population, and in a region fertile and beautiful. I tried to induce others to buy lands there, parcel out and give facilities for a self-sustaining community. No one would do so. My own patrimony was spent. By my wife selling what land she had in a free State (where there was progress) and myself borrowing five hundred dollars, we could then secure there for the purpose suggested, 130 acres of land. Knowing that the investment must be relatively and largely a sinking fund, we secured the land, and divided it into lots and small tracts.

Forty-two families have now their own homes there, and thus give home patronage to school and church. The Academy has 107 acres of land, and two good buildings. A charter has been secured from the State Legislature for the village and the Academy. Some man or woman could now do a good work there by building up a good industrial department.

CHAPTER VIII.

Return to Berea.-Resumption of the Work.-The American Missionary Association.-Work Denominational-Divisive.-Association of Ministers and Churches.-Kentucky Missionary Association.-A Convention of Christians.-An Address, "Wherein We Differ from the Denominations."

AT THE close of the war I came back to Berea and gave most of my time and strength to the work of helping to build up the school and church at Berea. This work has been sheltered and prospered. The College has ample grounds, good buildings, and an endowment of a hundred and six thousand dollars. Most of the time for the past fifteen years there have been here from three to four hundred pupils. Of these not less than one hundred and fifty go out each year to take charge of as many schools. These teachers impart the sentiments they have here imbibed and thus become a leavening, moulding influence throughout the land.

The church here, numbering now some two hundred and twenty-three members, is the one church of the place-now as from the beginning, in the year 1853, undenominational and unsectarian. Here those converted from the world, colored and white, together with those who once were Methodists, Baptists, Presbyterians, Congregationalists or Disciples, drop their denominational and divisive names, unite on Christ, and thus constitute the one church of the place. Hundreds go out from this place as one in Christ to carry this gospel of love and unity to others.

We believe that God by his Word and Spirit and his providence, has led to this unity, as it existed in the primitive church. We have been jealous of, and have repeatedly resisted and sloughed off, any and every denominational or ecclesiastical encroachment that might in any wise hinder the divine plan. This will be seen from further efforts and actions.

The American Missionary Association, with which I had been for many years associated, had in its early history been undenominational. In the year 1865 the Association was adopted by Congregationalists as an agency and society of that denomination, and the Association accepted the adoption, thus forsaking those who in the past had aided in its organization and growth, and in part, at least, because of its undenominational character. The Association is now in its official reports declared to be "the left wing of the Congregational corps" (see report, 1872)-also "as one of two Congregational missionary societies in the South," the A. M. A. and the A. H. M. S., and that "this association, debarred from its distinctive work at the first, wisely began efforts of its own." This "distinctive work of church planting" began in 1867. (See report of 1883.) "It was not a felt want of the South that there should be planted another denomination." The secretaries of the A. M. A. said:

"Our Congregational churches, whilst it is important to plant them, are not the first need. They can enter but slowly. The people do not appreciate them nor ask for them." (See report for December, 1882.) They might have added that, except in the cities or where there was a large Northern population such churches have been very small. The truth is, that Congregationalism, like Methodism or Presbyterianism, is a sect, a part of the body, named and recognized as such; not worse than others, but one of them. The churches in this denomination have their creeds, and these, as a rule, are sectarian, so uniformly so that the national council at Burial Hill declared: "We are Calvinistic in our faith." Samuel Wolcot says: "The Methodists receive what is called the Arminian system; we the Calvinistic." Joseph E. Roy, secretary of the American Missionary Association, in his Manual for Congregational Churches, says: "We adhere to the faith of the primitive churches held by our fathers and substantially embodied in the confessions and platforms as set forth in the synods of 1648 and 1680." These platforms are intensely Calvinistic. Again, he says we are "one branch of Christ's people, adhering to our peculiar faith and order." Again he says, "Congregationalists hold that baptism should be given to the infant children of believers." (P. 13.) The National Council of churches appointed a committee of twenty-one eminent divines, to draft a creed and confession to be submitted to the Congregational churches. That part of the eleventh article thus prepared, which refers to baptism, reads as follows: "We believe that baptism is to be administered to believers and their children." Joseph Cook regarded this creed as divisive. He said: "It would shut out Dr. Hackett, Pres. Wayland and thousands of others." This creed had a national endorsement at the National Council at Worcester, Mass., in 1890. Certain delegates from Georgia were accepted because it was declared that "they have adopted our creed and our polity." It proves nothing to say that Congregationalists are less sectarian than others. It is not the amount of evil, but the fact that an evil principle is supported. We have long since known that it was the moderate slaveholders that made slavery respectable.

I had in 1847 withdrawn from the Presbyterian church because of its persistent connection with slaveholding, and in the same year refused aid from the Home Missionary Society because of its persistent support of slaveholding churches;-and for the same reason the founders of the American Missionary Association withdrew their support and all association with that society. And now I feel that I must refuse all aid from the American Association because of its support of *sectarianism*, and its aggressive work in building up denominationalism; confessedly a great wrong, a great hindrance to truth and righteousness.

I said, too, "Congregationalism, like the other denominations, is an ecclesiasticism, having more or less control over its ministers and churches. In the language of its own authorities: 'Congregationalists do not approve of the name

Independents, and are abhorrent to such principles of independency as would shut them from giving an account of their matters to neighboring churches regularly demanding it of them.' 'Congregationalism is a communion of churches bound together by ties similar to those which bind together members of a single church.' All this designates a party-associated on opinions to which all believers could not subscribe. As such it is a division in the body of our Lord."

I said, "The division of Christians into sects and denominations is contrary to the letter and the spirit of the Gospel, a hindrance to reforms, and to the greatest progress of Christ's kingdom. As such, I may not bid it Godspeed." It was said to me, "Neither you nor the local church need take the name of Congregationalist-stand as you are." But I replied, "While I do not question your motives nor depreciate the good work you are able to accomplish, in some respects, I cannot approve of your methods. I shall be reported in the Congregational Year Book; and as receiving your aid. It would not be acting in good faith with you or with my own conscience to accept your beneficence and protest against your policy as radically wrong." I declined the aid of the Association. We are not "Congregationalist"-we accept no denominational arrangement or title.

THE ASSOCIATION OF MINISTERS AND CHURCHES.

Some of us who were workers here in Berea went, though with expressed objections, into another effort for what we then conceived might be necessary to the maintenance of truth and the highest efficiency. We formed "an Association of Ministers and Churches," bound together by a constitution which, though on a very catholic basis, was nevertheless an ecclesiasticism and a departure from what now seems to us the primitive order, and which involved church responsibilities. The objections to this arrangement were set forth in an article in the Berea *Evangelist*, and in the following words:

1. An "Association of Ministers and Churches" is a departure from the primitive order. The primitive order was to leave each church strictly independent. Each local church chose its own officers, disciplined its own offenders, and tried its own teachers. The local church, after the canon of Scripture was established, was the sole judge of fitness of order, of doctrine,-no space left for hierarchies or ecclesiasticisms. The divine pattern was complete and sufficient. This seems to us the New Testament doctrine, and while we do not make its acceptance a condition of our fellowship, it ought at least to be a rule for our own conduct.

2. Organizing "ministers and churches"-a class-into an association, on a basis which, however

catholic, if the usage prevails of extending the immunities and privileges of the Association only to those who are members of the body, and only to such members of the churches as are delegates, shows that the Association is a sect,-separated from others; then they become a clan.

Individual Christians may come up from all parts of the district, meet in convention, deliberate and devise, and return to their respective homes or churches, and not be a clan.

3. By organizing as an "Association of Ministers and Churches" we incur associate responsibilities, and guilt, if crime is persistently fellowshipped in the Association. God holds churches responsible for the conduct of their members. (1 Cor. v:13: 2 John II; Rev. 2:14.) Not individual ministers only, but churches, are members of the Association, and we, as members of the body, are responsible for their conduct in bidding God speed to wrong doers,-such as swear to conceal crime, take blasphemous oaths, and expurgate the name of Christ from the Scriptures they use, or the prayers they offer in their lodges. Some of the churches of the Association we then had, held and received such persons to their membership. But if individuals or churches are not constituent parts, then they are not responsible for each other's actions. If one or a dozen individual members of a church should, of their own accord, go to a Christian convention, and the convention should do any wrong or unwise thing, the church of which those individuals are members would not be responsible. These individuals would not go as

delegates, or representatives, or agents of the church. But if that church should be an integral part of an ecclesiastical association, and send to a meeting of this association delegates as representatives,-agents,-for the church, then the church would be responsible for the acts of the association so long as it should continue fellowship with it; and if the association, or any part of the churches composing it, should commit sin, all the members of the association would be partakers of the sin so long as the should fellowship the sinner.

The Association of Churches and Minister was abandoned. Most of the members favored the calling of conventions of individual Christians, to promote mutual fellowship and to extend the work of evangelization. Such a convention was called and adopted the plan for a missionary association presented in the following circular:

THE CHRISTIAN MISSIONARY ASSOCIATION OF KENTUCKY.

The reader will ask, Why another organization? We answer, that while the religion denominations, and the missionary societies that represent them, seek to convert men to Christ, they make a distinction between denominational and Christian fellowship by appending doctrines, polities and characteristics not essential to Christian life and character. Such a distinction is manifestly unwarranted by the Word of God, is contrary to the command of the apostle, "that there be no schism in the body" (1 Cor. 12: 25), and the prayer of our Saviour, "that they may all be one" (John 17: 21). Such denominational divisions beget weakness, and tempt men for sake of numbers to receive to their fellowship persons living in un-Christ-like practices, such as connection with the secret lodge system, the use, manufacture and sale of intoxicating drinks, and the spirit and practice of caste in the "household of faith." Because so many Christians have been "carnal and walk as men," they have separated those whom God hath joined together, and divided the Body wherein "there is neither Greek nor Jew, circumcision nor uncircumcision, Barbarian, Scythian, bond nor free, but Christ is all and in all."

There are in Kentucky and other States, churches that are now, and for years have been, separate from these denominational organizations and un-Christ-like practices. They need aid in pastoral support and in their efforts to extend the Gospel. They propose no separation from the whole family of Christ nor even an association with each other as a distinctive body. They find no warrant for a separate association of churches in the Word of God, and believe that such separate associations tend only to a forbidden schism in the body of our Lord.

The Christian Missionary Association which asks your aid, is made up not of churches, a such, but of individuals. This association has been regularly incorporated, as an association by the Legislature of Kentucky. This Association, at their regular meetings, will hear reports, audit accounts, vote appropriations, appoint missionaries, and an executive board to aid in its objects, who also may send out laborers and who shall supervise the work of evangelization.

This association seeks the unification of a believers in Christ, and their united opposition to all known iniquity. We aim to conserve the material and moral resources of the church by bringing together, as far as practicable, all Christians in any given locality, on the basis of a common unity in Christ. Whilst we shall give aid to those seeking the suppression of the use of and traffic in intoxicating drinks, and in opposing all secret orders, we shall especially seek to send out and assist those evangelists who shall preach Christ in all the fullness of his character, baptizing all thus converted into his name, and organizing them into undenominational churches, whose only head is the Lord Jesus Christ. The present Executive Board is located at Berea, Madison County, Kentucky, and will receive and disburse all funds as directed by the donor.

J. G. FEE, President. H. H. HINMAN, Cor. Sec'y. ALFRED TITUS, Rec. Sec'y. JAMES VAN WINKLE, Rec. Sec'y. S. G. HANSON, Treas.

The readers will see in all these efforts there has been a continuous purpose to have the church free from all complicity with wrong doing,-have it free from all ecclesiasticisms that embarrass the utterance of truth, or hinder reforms and involve associate responsibility or guilt,-an effort to plant churches as planted by our Lord and his apostles,- independent and undenominational. The divine pattern will yet be found to be the wisest and most efficient. Perhaps, on this point, I can do the reader no better service than by directing his attention to an address the writer delivered before the Christian convention held in Dayton, Ohio, May 21-23, 1890.

AN ADDRESS, BY JOHN G. FEE.

Delivered before the late Christian Union Convention. held in Dayton, Ohio, May 21-23, 1890.

The object of this convention, as set forth in the call, is to suggest ways and devise means by which to secure the visible union of all true Christians in any given locality, as the one church of that locality; and this union on the basis of manifested faith in the Lord Jesus Christ, the Son of God, as the Saviour from sin.

As announced in the programme, I propose to show "wherein this movement differs from the denominations around us."

All the denominations, in all that is peculiar to them as such, begin with opinions-opinions about a doctrine, about a rite, a polity, and in their distinctive work build upon these opinions. We begin with and build upon a person,-the Lord Jesus Christ, the Son of God, the Saviour from sin; and "other foundations can no man lay"

That Jesus Christ, the Son of the living God, came into the world to save sinners, is the creed of the Gospel.

Belief on him is the condition of salvation. "Believe in the Lord Jesus Christ and thou shalt be saved."

Manifested faith in him, as the Saviour from sin, is the reason for fellowship and co-operation.

This faith in a person, the Lord Jesus Christ, induced as it is by the truth and Spirit of God, carries with it a radical change in the believer; an entire conformity of will, of affection, of life to the Lord Jesus.

This is seen from the very import of the original word (*Pisteuo*), translated "believe." This word implies not mere intellectual assent to a fact, even the fact that Jesus is the Son of God, but the word, when used to designate faith in, or belief on a person, implies more: it implies committal. This is so clearly true that the word is sometimes translated commit, "Jesus, knowing the hearts of all men, committed not himself to them." John 2:24.

The soul that thus believes on, commits itself to the Lord Jesus, opens the door of the heart to Christ, and in so doing becomes "a new creature." Pertinent are the words of the apostle, "He that believeth that Jesus is the Christ" (commits himself to Jesus as the Christ) "is born of God."

Such a believer is more than a mere moralist; more than a mere humanitarian; more than a mere professor; he is "a new creature."

Opinions about a doctrine, a rite or a polity, however correct, carry with them no such radical change of heart and character; no sense of forgiveness, peace and joy in the Holy Ghost.

Again, this faith in Christ is simple; a child can comprehend it; a child knows what faith in a person is. It can believe on and trust in a parent or a friend. Also a child exercising this faith can have a conscious experience and can tell that experience,- can tell that it trusts in Jesus as its Saviour. But this child, whilst it can confess, trust in Jesus, and be fitted for baptism and a place in the visible Church of Christ, cannot say it understands the five points of Calvinism, nor the twenty-five articles of Methodist Discipline, nor the thirty-nine articles of the Episcopal Church.

Again, this faith in Christ is all comprehensive, secures all moral excellence. Faith in Christ, belief on him, is committal to him who is holy, harmless and undefiled, the one "in whom dwells all the fullness of the God-head bodily." This faith then secures all moral excellence. Not so with mere opinions; they have no transforming power.

The devils believe facts concerning Christ; give intellectual assent, but no committal to Christ, and are devils still. Many of the slaveholders were orthodox, "sound in the faith," in the sense of opinion, but were still monsters of iniquity.

Whilst it will be conceded that faith in a person, the Lord Jesus Christ, is simple and comprehensive, the question will be asked, "What about baptism and all good works?" We reply, the soul that believes on Christ (commits itself to him) must, from the very nature of the case, obey Christ,-in baptism, in all things commanded by him, must conform readily to his entire life; and thus in the word and the life of the living person, have a moral standard in the light of which to test the character of secret orders, caste spirit, intemperate habits, all individual acts and social customs. Thus the creed we avow is divine, simple, and all comprehensive.

It will be said the denominations have this creed and this faith in Christ in common with you. True; but they add to the divine plan-add something else; and build distinctively on this something else. They "lay other foundations" as the basis of fellowship and co-operation, and whilst they recognize true believers as Christians, they co-operate ecclesiastically only with those of certain opinions, and thus build parties, sects. Every denomination is an illustration of the fact stated. We begin with the Lutheran. A bit of history will vivify the illustration.

For the first thirteen years of the Reformation Protestants were undivided. They had union on Christ. D'Aubigne says there existed at that time in the evangelical body no sects, hatred or schisms;

Christian unity was a reality. The renewed disciples of Christ presented themselves to the Pope, to the emperor, to the world and to the scaffold as forming one body. Carlstadt, speaking of Protestants, said, "We are but one body, one house, one people; we live and die by one and the same Saviour."

There was union on Christ but difference in opinion in what Zwingle termed "secondary matters." Luther and Zwingle differed in opinion about the eucharist, the Lord's Supper. At the conference at Marburg, Luther said, "I believe that Christ's body is in heaven, and that Christ's body is in the bread, as the sword is in the scabbard." * * "The sacrament of the altar is the sacrament of the very body and the very blood of Jesus Christ." This opinion of actual presence he reaffirmed at Augsburg, Smalcald, and at Wittemburg. At the latter he added, as a modification, the phrase "spiritual manducation." To this modified opinion he prefixed other opinions about depravity, original sin, inability and imputation. With these opinions, which he afterward again modified, he formed a creed for a party, which party soon took a name by which to designate the party from the rest of the body. Thus began sects and denominations early in the Reformation.

Lutheranism has undergone many modifications in different countries and at different times. These frequent modifications of the creed, like the continued modifications of the creeds of all other denominations, show that these creeds are but the fluctuating opinions of men. The divine creed changes not.

Another illustration of the fact that the denominations begin with and build upon opinions may be drawn from the Presbyterian denomination. The brethren in this denomination are of the opinion that the government of the Church should be by elders; that the authority of their ministers to preach the Gospel, administer the ordinances and feed the flock, is through the Holy Ghost by the imposition of the hands of the Presbytery.

These Presbyterian brethren are also of the opinion that the five points of Calvinism are the correct interpretation of certain portions of the Word of God. With this polity and with these opinions of doctrine they form a creed and build a party upon it.

The denomination known as Congregationalists present another illustration. Congregationalists are of the opinion that the government of the local church should be by the congregation; that local churches should be in ecclesiastical fellowship, united in associations or councils. (See report of Committee of the National Council in 1889.)

For a creed, Congregationalists first adopted the Savoy platform; then in this country, after a time, adopted the Cambridge platform-both platforms are intensely Calvinistic. In the National Council of 1865 the Congregationalists there declared that their faith, as a denomination, "is Calvinistic." The creed drafted by the commission appointed by the

National Council in 1884 is a modified creed of twelve articles,-articles which many Christians cannot accept. A clause in the eleventh article affirms that "baptism is to be administered to believers and their children," a clause which Joseph Cook said would exclude Francis Wayland, Dr. Hackett and thousands of other Christians.

The creed received a national sanction at the recent meeting at Worcester, Mass., where, as a reason for receiving delegates from the State of Georgia, it was said "they accept our polity and adhere to the creed set forth by our Commission in 1884." Thus Congregationalism has its polity, its association of churches and its amended creed,-a creed built upon the shifting opinions of men and the distinctive features of a party.

The formation of the Methodist denomination affords another illustration. For some fifteen years before our Revolutionary war, vigorous missionary efforts were carried on in several of the Southern States of this Union under the labors of Wesley, Whitfield and others. The converts worshipped for a time, not as a denomination, but in local churches or societies; some of them simply with Wesley's rules. Efforts were made to form a denomination. These were as often resisted. At length, in 1784, under the labors of Coke and Asbury, a convention was called, a proposition for a distinct ecclesiastical association was submitted and accepted. Twenty-four articles of faith, with an episcopal form of government, and the name of Methodist Episcopal as that by which to designate the body, was also accepted. The polity, the name, and a fourth part of the articles of faith were then and now are such that thousands of Christians cannot accept them; they are divisive. The denomination, like other denominations, is built upon opinions, and is a schism in the body of Christ.

The Baptist denomination presents another illustration. The Baptist brethren are of the opinion that the original Greek word, Baptizo, when used to designate action, means immerse; and should have been translated so in our version; and that the right of baptism should be administered only to believers.

This, after much care and study, is my own opinion, and I act accordingly,-strive to live up to my convictions. Here I must stop, for I recognize the fact that in our version we have not a translation of the original word, but only the original Greek word, with an English termination affixed. I also recognize the fact that ninety and nine out of every hundred true believers are unable to translate; and that they must of necessity interpret. As a Protestant, as a brother, I must grant to manifest believers the right of private interpretation; especially when it is conceded that the mistake in interpretation may be consistent with Christian life and character.

I believe our Pedo-baptist brethren have made a mistake in their act of confession and consecration, but they have nevertheless made confession and consecration, though they have erred in the form of the act. The mistake in the manner of action does not destroy Christian character,-evidence of true faith in Christ as the Saviour from sin. Again, my belief is that our Pedo-baptist brethren, in their act of consecration, have omitted an important feature of a true baptism; the symbolization of "death to sin and resurrection to newness of life"; nevertheless, by their trust in Christ they have the fact, death to sin and resurrection to a new life. They have failed, as I believe, to symbolize the fact.

It is my opinion that my Pedo-baptist brethren have omitted the impressive emblem of the death, burial and resurrection of our Lord; but I know that from other sources in God's Word they do teach these precious facts.

It will be said, you insist upon correct opinions about Christ; why not about the word baptize? I reply, I do believe and teach, as revealed in God's Word, that Christ is the "eternal life," and not a secondary or after existence; that he is the "Word who was with God and was God"-"God manifest in the flesh"; but the thing I insist upon is not opinion about Christ, but the actual fact of trust in committal to him as the personal Saviour from sin. This is vital to life and character; but correct opinions about the import of the word baptize, or the design of baptism, are not vital in the case of the true believer; the mistake does not destroy Christian character.

With Alex. Campbell we concur when he says, "There are Christians among the sects." We think it is best to treat these Christians as such; believing that if anxious inquirers shall be freed from the bias of sects and denominational teachings, they will generally apprehend the truth of God's Word in reference to the action and design of baptism. Our Baptist brethren, however, are of the opinion that church fellowship should be extended only to immersed believers; and upon this opinion form a party, and take a name by which to distinguish the party from the rest of the body.

What we have said of the denominations previously referred to, is true of all other denominations, even of those who have no written creed, or those who call themselves by the Catholic name "Christians." A creed may be as real when oral, as when written. We may take an illustration- opposition to the doctrine of the Trinity, or the doctrine of the "distinct personality of the Son from the Father," or baptism for the remission of sins, or immersion of a believer as a condition of fellowship and co-operation, and make acceptance of any one of these opinions the condition of fellowship and co-operation, and then take some name by which to designate the association, and you will have the essential elements of a denomination, though there be no written creed.

The Catholic name "Christian" does not alter the nature of the association. The name Christian may be prostituted from its high purpose of designating Christian character,-a follower or followers of Christ, to that of designating a party,-a part of the body of Christ, *separated on an opinion not necessary* to oneness in Christ, This may be with or without an association of churches.

The error, then, of denominationalism is in taking an opinion about some doctrine, rite or polity, and making a party on that opinion, rite or polity, and taking a name, however Catholic, by which to designate that party from the rest of the body of Christ.

The question will be asked, "Is not the local church you advocate a section, a part of the body, and that, too, with a name by which to designate it?"

We reply, yes; but not in the reprehensible sense of the word; the sense condemned by the Word of God. It is right that the followers of Christ be separated from the *world*,-be in this respect a *section*, and that the church thus separated wear the name of Christ, its head.

Whilst, then, the true followers of Christ are, by their new birth, their baptism, their worship, their lives, separated from the world, they are not to be separated *one from another*, they are to be one body, wearing the one name,-the name of Christ, their head. But the division of the body of believers into sects, parties, and this on mere opinions about doctrines, rites or polities, with names by which to designate these separate parties, is not right. Such separation is the *sin of schism*, condemned by the Word of God, and deplored by good men and women. We then build on Christ, a person, and seek to convert men to him in all the fullness of his character, baptize in his name, and gather together for worship and thus constitute the one church of the locality; not as a party, but as a *part of* the whole body of Christ, wearing his name, and his name only.

For evangelization we may have Mission Boards appointed by conventions composed of individuals, and thus be as undenominational as the American Bible Society itself.

This board, or executive committee, may receive funds, commission evangelists and teachers, who shall devote themselves to the one great work of converting souls to Christ in all the fullness of his character.

Then will the church "come up out of the wilderness, leaning upon the arm of her beloved, fair as the morn, clear as the sun, and terrible as an army with banners."

THE END.

Made in the USA
Coppell, TX
08 December 2019

12616121R00092